Southern Living
Quick and Easy
Weeknight Meals™

Dear Friends,

As a working mom with two teenagers, I face the challenges of work, carpools, and homework just like you. I'm guilty of rushing to the store after work, wandering the aisles, and wondering what to serve for supper. That's why I'm so pleased to bring you these wonderful recipes, perfect for busy days.

In these pages, you'll find 314 recipes that include all our best time-saving tips, from slow-cooker dinners to make-ahead meals. Check out our section of top-rated favorites on page 67. These are what I like to call people-always-ask-me-for-the-recipe recipes. You (and your friends) will love them.

Because we understand how busy you are, our "Meals in Minutes" chapter (starting on page 4) groups recipes by the amount of time they take to prepare. Throughout the book, we tell you how much time you'll need to prepare each dish and what can be made ahead of time.

I hope these recipes make your life a little easier at suppertime, as they have mine. Happy cooking!

Vicki

Vicki A. Poellnitz
Editor

Oxmoor House®

Southern Living
Quick and Easy
Weeknight Meals

EDITOR: Vicki A. Poellnitz
ART DIRECTOR: Claudia Hon
COPY CHIEF: Paula Hunt Hughes
COPY EDITORS: Rhonda Richards, Ryan Wallace
PRODUCTION COORDINATOR: Christy Coleman
FOODS EDITOR: Shannon Sliter Satterwhite
SENIOR WRITERS: Donna Florio, Andria Scott Hurst
ASSOCIATE FOODS EDITORS: Natalie Brown, Charla Draper, Shirley Harrington, Holley Johnson, Kate Nicholson, Mary Allen Perry
ASSISTANT RECIPE EDITOR: Ashley Leath
TEST KITCHENS DIRECTOR: Lyda Jones Burnette   **ASSISTANT TEST KITCHENS DIRECTOR:** James Schend
TEST KITCHENS SPECIALIST/FOOD STYLING: Vanessa McNeil Rocchio
TEST KITCHENS PROFESSIONALS: Marian Cooper Cairns, Rebecca Kracke Gordon, Pam Lolley, Angela Sellers
SENIOR PHOTOGRAPHERS: Ralph Anderson, Van Chaplin, Joseph De Sciose, Art Meripol, John O'Hagan, Charles Walton IV
PHOTOGRAPHERS: Jim Bathie, Mary Margaret Chambliss, Gary Clark, Tina Cornett, William Dickey, Beth Dreiling, Laurey W. Glenn, Meg McKinney
SENIOR PHOTO STYLIST: Buffy Hargett   **ASSOCIATE PHOTO STYLIST:** Alan Henderson
PHOTO STYLISTS: Lisa Powell Bailey, Rose Nguyen, Cari South, Amy P. Wilson
PHOTO LIBRARIAN: Tracy Duncan   **PHOTO PRODUCTION MANAGER:** Larry Hunter
PHOTO SERVICES: Amanda Leigh Abbett, Ginny P. Allen, Catherine Carr

SOUTHERN LIVING
EDITOR IN CHIEF: John Alex Floyd, Jr.
MANAGING EDITOR: Clay Nordan
EXECUTIVE EDITORS: Derick Belden, Scott Jones, Warner McGowin, Dianne Young
CREATIVE DIRECTOR: Jon Thompson
DEPUTY EDITOR: Kenner Patton
COPY CHIEF: Dawn P. Cannon
PRODUCTION AND COLOR QUALITY MANAGER: Katie Terrell Morrow
CREATIVE DEVELOPMENT DIRECTOR: Valerie Fraser Luesse
DIRECTOR OF PHOTOGRAPHY: Mark Sandlin
ASSISTANT TO THE EDITOR IN CHIEF: Marian Cooper   **OFFICE MANAGER:** Wanda T. Stephens
ADMINISTRATIVE ASSISTANTS: Chris Carrier Garmon, Lynne Long, Sandra J. Thomas
EDITORIAL ASSISTANTS: Karen Brechin, Catherine K. Russell, Pat York
ASSISTANT ART DIRECTOR: Gae Watson
SENIOR DESIGNERS: Chris Hoke, Patricia See Hooten, Jennie McClain Shannon
DESIGNER/ILLUSTRATOR: Christopher Davis
SENIOR COPY EDITOR: Julia Pittard Coker
COPY EDITORS: Katie Bowlby, Stephanie Gibson Mims, Libby Monteith Minor, Cindy Riegle, JoAnn Weatherly
COPY ASSISTANTS: Tara Ivey, Marilyn R. Smith
ASSISTANT PRODUCTION MANAGER: Jamie Barnhart
PRODUCTION COORDINATORS: Paula Dennis, Brooke Krannich
EDITORIAL CONTRIBUTORS: Ashley Arthur, Emily C. Beaumont, Mindi Shapiro Levine

OXMOOR HOUSE, INC.
EDITOR IN CHIEF: Nancy Fitzpatrick Wyatt
EXECUTIVE EDITOR: Susan Carlisle Payne
ART DIRECTOR: Keith McPherson
MANAGING EDITOR: Allison Long Lowery
EDITOR: Julie Gunter
COPY EDITOR: Jacqueline Giovanelli
EDITORIAL ASSISTANT: Amelia Heying
SENIOR DESIGNER: Emily Albright Parrish
CONTRIBUTING DESIGNER: Amy Bickell
DIRECTOR OF PRODUCTION: Laura Lockhart
PRODUCTION MANAGER: Theresa Beste Farley
PRODUCTION ASSISTANT: Faye Porter Bonner

Southern Living At HOME®
PRESIDENT: John H. McIntosh, Jr.
VICE PRESIDENT AND GENERAL MANAGER: Laura Taylor
DIRECTOR OF MARKETING AND FIELD DEVELOPMENT: Gary Wright
RESEARCH MANAGER: Jon Williams

Created exclusively for *Southern Living At HOME®*, the Direct Selling Company of Southern Progress Corporation. For information about *Southern Living At HOME,* please write to: Consultant Support, P.O. Box 830951, Birmingham, AL 35283-0951, or visit southernlivingathome.com

To order additional publications, call 1-800-765-6400.
For more books to enrich your life, visit **oxmoorhouse.com**

To search, savor, and share thousands of recipes, visit **myrecipes.com**

ON THE COVER: *Cilantro-Garlic Sirloin With Zesty Corn Salsa (page 34) pairs well with Roasted Onion Salad and Garlic Vinaigrette (page 6). Photography Ralph Anderson, styling Buffy Hargett, food styling Angela Sellers*

75

9

21

106

18

Contents

Meals in Minutes

This choice collection of streamlined dishes—ready in less than 30, 45, or 60 minutes—will ease the burden of what to cook tonight, based on the amount of time you have.

To speed up menu planning, you'll find recipes for poultry, pork, beef, and seafood entrées as well as vegetable sides, salads, and breads in this section. Here's help in getting supper on the table.

Superfast Meals
You can make the busiest of evenings almost effortless.

Chicken With Fresh Herbs and Vegetables

You *can* have supper ready in half an hour or less. These recipes, including entrées and sides, are perfect choices for evenings when you know you'll have limited time. They also come to the rescue when you need to cook a meal on short notice.

Chicken With Fresh Herbs and Vegetables

MAKES 4 SERVINGS
PREP: 10 MIN., COOK: 21 MIN.
Serve over rice or linguine for a one-dish meal. If you don't have fresh herbs, substitute 1 Tbsp. dried basil and 1 tsp. dried oregano.

¼ cup fine, dry breadcrumbs
6 Tbsp. shredded Parmesan cheese, divided
4 skinned and boned chicken breasts
2 Tbsp. olive oil
10 large mushrooms, quartered
1 large green bell pepper, thinly sliced
3 large tomatoes, coarsely chopped
1 large garlic clove, pressed
½ tsp. salt
¼ cup chopped fresh basil
1 Tbsp. chopped fresh oregano

1. Combine breadcrumbs and 4 Tbsp. Parmesan cheese, and dredge chicken in mixture.
2. Cook chicken in hot oil in a large skillet over medium-high heat 4 minutes on each side or until browned. Remove chicken from skillet.
3. Add mushrooms and bell pepper to skillet; sauté 3 minutes. Add tomatoes, garlic, and salt; return chicken to skillet. Cover, reduce heat, and simmer 10 minutes. Stir in basil, oregano, and remaining 2 Tbsp. Parmesan cheese. Serve immediately.

Creamy Pork Chops

MAKES 4 TO 6 SERVINGS
PREP: 10 MIN., COOK: 17 MIN.

¼ cup all-purpose flour
¾ tsp. salt, divided
½ tsp. pepper
8 boneless breakfast pork chops
2 Tbsp. vegetable oil
¼ cup white vinegar
1 (8-oz.) container sour cream
2 Tbsp. sugar
⅛ tsp. ground cloves
2 bay leaves
1 Tbsp. chopped fresh parsley (optional)

1. Combine flour, ½ tsp. salt, and pepper. Dredge pork chops in flour mixture.
2. Cook pork chops in hot oil in a large skillet over high heat 5 minutes on each side or until golden. Remove pork chops from skillet.
3. Add vinegar, and cook 2 minutes, stirring to loosen particles from bottom of skillet. Stir in sour cream, next 3 ingredients, and remaining ¼ tsp. salt; simmer 5 minutes. Remove and discard bay leaves; pour sauce over pork chops. Sprinkle with parsley, if desired. ▶

Roasted Onion Salad and
Garlic Vinaigrette

Roasted Onion Salad

MAKES 8 SERVINGS
PREP: 15 MIN., BROIL: 10 MIN.,
STAND: 5 MIN.

When broiling, be sure to check the onions after five minutes to prevent overbrowning.

5 medium-size sweet onions, cut
   into ½-inch-thick slices
2 Tbsp. olive oil
Salt and pepper to taste
8 cups gourmet mixed salad
   greens
½ cup chopped walnuts, toasted
   (optional)
1 (4-oz.) package crumbled blue
   cheese (optional)
Garlic Vinaigrette

1. Arrange onion slices on an aluminum foil-lined baking sheet. Brush evenly with olive oil. Sprinkle evenly with salt and pepper to taste.
2. Broil 5 inches from heat 10 minutes or until onion slices are lightly browned.

Let onion slices stand 5 minutes.
3. Combine salad greens, and, if desired, walnuts and blue cheese; toss gently. Top with onion slices; drizzle with Garlic Vinaigrette.

Garlic Vinaigrette:
MAKES 1 CUP
PREP: 10 MIN.

3 garlic cloves, coarsely chopped
2 shallots, coarsely chopped
¼ cup chopped fresh parsley
2 Tbsp. white wine vinegar
½ tsp. dried crushed red pepper
½ tsp. salt
½ tsp. freshly ground black pepper
⅔ cup olive oil

1. Pulse chopped garlic and shallots in a food processor 3 or 4 times. Add chopped parsley and next 4 ingredients; process 20 seconds, stopping once to scrape down sides. With processor running, gradually pour ⅔ cup olive oil in a slow, steady stream through food chute until blended.

Rice Pilaf

MAKES 4 SERVINGS
PREP: 5 MIN., COOK: 10 MIN.

1 (8-oz.) package sliced
   mushrooms
1 (6-oz.) package quick-cooking
   long-grain and wild rice mix
1 tsp. vegetable oil
1 (14-oz.) can vegetable broth

1. Sauté mushrooms and long-grain and wild rice in hot oil in a medium saucepan over medium-high heat for 5 minutes.
2. Stir in broth and rice seasoning packet; bring to a boil. Cover, reduce heat, and simmer 5 minutes.
Kitchen Express: Microwave 1 (8-oz.) package sliced mushrooms in a medium-size microwave-safe bowl at HIGH 5 minutes; drain well. Heat 2 (8.8-oz.) pouches ready-to-serve long-grain and wild rice mix according to package directions. Stir together rice mix and mushrooms.

Balsamic Pork Chops

MAKES 6 SERVINGS
PREP: 10 MIN., COOK: 20 MIN.

1 (6.2-oz) box quick-cooking
   long-grain and wild rice mix
3 Tbsp. all-purpose flour
1 tsp. chopped fresh rosemary
½ tsp. salt
½ tsp. pepper
6 (¾-inch-thick) boneless pork loin
   chops
2 Tbsp. butter or margarine
2 Tbsp. olive oil
2 garlic cloves, pressed
1 (14-oz.) can chicken broth
⅓ cup balsamic vinegar
Garnish: fresh rosemary sprigs

1. Cook rice according to package directions; keep warm.
2. Combine flour, 1 tsp. rosemary, ½ tsp. salt, and ½ tsp. pepper. Dredge pork chops in flour mixture.
3. Melt butter with oil in a large skillet over medium-high heat; add garlic, and sauté 1 minute. Add pork chops, and cook 4 minutes on each side or until golden. Remove pork chops.
4. Add broth and vinegar, stirring to loosen particles from bottom of skillet. Cook 6 minutes or until liquid is reduced by half. Add pork chops, and cook 5 minutes or until done. Serve over rice. Garnish, if desired.

Blue Cheese Potatoes

MAKES 4 SERVINGS
PREP: 5 MIN., BAKE: 25 MIN.
Experiment with other taste pairings. Use a favorite salad dressing-and-cheese combination to create your own new recipe.

1 (1-lb., 4-oz.) package refrigerated
   new potato wedges*
1 Tbsp. olive oil
½ cup refrigerated blue cheese
   dressing
¼ tsp. freshly ground black
   pepper
¼ cup crumbled blue cheese

1. Drizzle potatoes with oil, tossing to coat. Place potatoes evenly in 13- x 9-inch baking dish.
2. Bake at 450° for 25 minutes.
3. Transfer potatoes to a serving bowl. Toss with dressing and pepper. Sprinkle with cheese.
*1 lb., 4 oz. potatoes, peeled and cut into wedges, may be used.
Note: For testing purposes only, we used Simply Potatoes New Potato Wedges and Naturally Fresh Bleu Cheese Dressing.
Feta Cheese Potatoes: Substitute Ranch dressing for blue cheese dressing and crumbled feta cheese for crumbled blue cheese.

Greek Tomatoes

MAKES 6 SERVINGS
PREP: 5 MIN.

4 medium tomatoes, cut into
   ¼-inch-thick slices
¼ cup drained capers, rinsed
1 (4-oz.) package feta cheese,
   crumbled
¼ cup minced fresh parsley
Coarsely ground black pepper
2 Tbsp. olive oil

1. Place tomatoes on a platter. Sprinkle with capers and next 3 ingredients; drizzle evenly with oil. Serve immediately.▶

Balsamic Pork Chops

meals in minutes

Shrimp With Roasted Red Pepper Cream

MAKES 6 SERVINGS
PREP: 15 MIN., COOK: 8 MIN.

1 (7-oz.) package vermicelli
1 (12-oz.) jar roasted red bell
  peppers, drained
1 (8-oz.) package ⅓-less-fat cream
  cheese, softened
½ cup low-sodium fat-free chicken
  broth
3 garlic cloves, chopped
½ tsp. ground red pepper
2 lb. peeled cooked large shrimp
¼ cup chopped fresh basil
Garnish: fresh basil sprig

1. Prepare pasta according to package directions, omitting salt and oil. Drain and keep pasta warm.
2. Process red peppers and next 4 ingredients in a blender or food processor until smooth, scraping down sides. Pour mixture into a large skillet.
3. Cook over medium heat, stirring often, 5 minutes or until thoroughly heated. Add shrimp, and cook, stirring occasionally, 2 to 3 minutes or just until shrimp turn pink. Remove from heat. Serve over hot cooked pasta. Sprinkle with basil. Garnish, if desired.
Note: For testing purposes only, we used Alessi Sweet Pimento Italian Style Fire Roasted Peppers.

Garlic Bread

MAKES 8 SERVINGS
PREP: 5 MIN., BAKE: 20 MIN.,
STAND: 3 MIN.

½ cup butter or margarine,
  softened
2½ tsp. garlic powder
¾ tsp. Italian seasoning
½ tsp. dried oregano
¼ tsp. pepper
1 cup (4 oz.) shredded Italian
  three-cheese blend
1 (16-oz.) French bread loaf, split

1. Combine first 5 ingredients and ⅓ cup cheese; spread mixture evenly on cut sides of bread. Sprinkle evenly with ⅔ cup cheese. Place on a baking sheet.
2. Bake at 375° for 15 to 20 minutes or until cheese is melted and golden. Let stand 2 to 3 minutes before serving.

Fettuccine With Squash and Zucchini

MAKES 4 TO 6 SERVINGS
PREP: 15 MIN., COOK: 2 MIN.

12 oz. fettuccine
2 medium-size yellow squash, cut
  into thin strips
2 medium zucchini squash, cut into
  thin strips
1 Tbsp. vegetable oil
1 minced garlic clove
2 Tbsp. fresh basil, cut into thin strips
1 tsp. salt
½ tsp. pepper

1. Prepare fettuccine according to package directions. Keep warm.
2. Sauté vegetables in hot oil in a large Dutch oven over medium heat 1 minute. Stir in garlic and basil; sauté 1 more minute. Stir in salt and pepper.
3. Stir in warm fettuccine, tossing to combine.

Bistro Grilled Chicken Pizza

MAKES 6 SERVINGS
PREP: 15 MIN., GRILL: 10 MIN.
Use long-handled grilling tongs and a spatula to turn the dough with ease.

1 (13.8-oz.) can refrigerated pizza
  crust dough
1 tsp. olive oil
¾ cup pizza sauce
4 plum tomatoes, sliced
2 cups chopped cooked chicken
1 (4-oz.) package tomato-and-basil
  feta cheese
1 cup (4 oz.) shredded mozzarella
  cheese
2 Tbsp. chopped fresh basil

1. Unroll dough, and place on a lightly greased 18- x 12-inch sheet of heavy-duty aluminum foil. Starting at center, press out dough with hands to form a 13- x 9-inch rectangle. Brush dough evenly with olive oil.
2. Invert dough onto grill cooking grate; peel off foil. Grill, covered with grill lid, over medium heat (300° to 350°) 2 to 3 minutes or until bottom of dough is golden brown. Turn dough over, and grill, covered with grill lid, 1 to 2 minutes or until bottom is set. Carefully remove crust from grill to an aluminum foil-lined baking sheet.
3. Microwave pizza sauce in a small microwave-safe bowl at HIGH 30 seconds or until warm, stirring once. Spread sauce evenly over crust; top with tomatoes and chicken. Sprinkle evenly with cheeses and basil. Return pizza to cooking grate (pizza should slide off easily).
4. Grill, covered with grill lid, 3 to 5 more minutes or until crust is done and cheese is melted.

Shrimp With Roasted
Red Pepper Cream

Sesame-Ginger Chicken

Sesame-Ginger Chicken

MAKES 4 SERVINGS
PREP: 10 MIN., GRILL: 12 MIN.
Stir together just four tangy and sweet ingredients to baste on grilled Sesame-Ginger Chicken. Use kitchen shears to cut the green onion garnish.

1 Tbsp. sesame seeds, toasted
2 Tbsp. soy sauce
2 Tbsp. honey
2 tsp. grated fresh ginger
Vegetable cooking spray
4 skinned and boned chicken breasts
Mixed salad greens
Garnish: sliced green onions

1. Stir together toasted sesame seeds and next 3 ingredients.
2. Coat cooking grate with cooking spray; place on grill over medium-high heat (350° to 400°). Place chicken on grate; grill 6 minutes on each side or until done, basting often with sauce mixture. Serve over salad greens. Garnish, if desired.
Note: Soy sauce mixture may also be basted on pork.

Creamy Mac and Cheese

MAKES 4 TO 6 SIDE-DISH SERVINGS
PREP: 10 MIN., COOK: 8 MIN.

8 oz. elbow macaroni
1 (10-oz.) container refrigerated Alfredo sauce
½ cup milk
½ tsp. freshly ground black pepper
¼ tsp. salt
¼ tsp. ground red pepper
1 (8-oz.) block Cheddar cheese, shredded

1. Prepare pasta according to package directions. Drain and keep warm.
2. Bring Alfredo sauce and next 4 ingredients to a boil in a large saucepan. Remove from heat. Stir in cheese until melted. Stir in warm pasta. Serve immediately.

Pretzel Pork Chops

MAKES 6 SERVINGS
PREP: 15 MIN., COOK: 10 MIN.

6 (½-inch-thick) boneless pork chops, trimmed
¼ cup mayonnaise
½ tsp. garlic powder
½ cup crushed pretzels
2 tsp. butter or margarine
¼ tsp. dried sage

1. Place pork between 2 sheets of heavy-duty plastic wrap, and flatten to a ¼-inch thickness, using a meat mallet or rolling pin.
2. Stir together mayonnaise and garlic powder. Dip pork in mayonnaise mixture; dredge in crushed pretzels.
3. Melt butter in a large nonstick skillet over medium heat. Add pork chops; sprinkle evenly with sage. Cook 4 to 5 minutes on each side or until done.

Tomato-Red Onion Salad

MAKES 4 SERVINGS
PREP: 15 MIN., STAND: 10 MIN.
Create a variation of this salad by adding crumbled feta or goat cheese, kalamata olives, and sliced cucumbers.

4 medium tomatoes, cut into ¼-inch-thick slices
¼ small red onion, thinly sliced
2 Tbsp. chopped fresh oregano
2 Tbsp. olive oil
1 Tbsp. red wine vinegar
¼ tsp. salt
⅛ tsp. pepper

1. Layer tomatoes and onion slices on a serving platter. Sprinkle evenly with chopped fresh oregano.
2. Whisk together oil, vinegar, salt, and pepper. Drizzle evenly over tomato and onion slices. Let stand 10 minutes before serving.

Lemon Mashed Potatoes

MAKES 4 SERVINGS
PREP: 5 MIN., COOK: 12 MIN.

1 (22-oz.) package frozen mashed potatoes
¼ cup butter or margarine
1 tsp. lemon rind
¾ tsp. salt
¼ to ½ tsp. freshly ground black pepper

1. Prepare potatoes according to package directions. Stir in butter and remaining ingredients. Serve immediately. ▶

meals in minutes

Cucumber Salad With Roasted Red Bell Pepper Dressing

MAKES 6 SERVINGS
PREP: 10 MIN.

This recipe comes together in a flash. Store the dressing in the refrigerator up to one week.

8 cups gourmet salad greens
2 cucumbers, thinly sliced
1 small red onion, thinly sliced
Roasted Red Bell Pepper Dressing

1. Combine salad greens, sliced cucumbers, and onion; serve with Roasted Red Bell Pepper Dressing.

Roasted Red Bell Pepper Dressing:

MAKES ABOUT 2 CUPS
PREP: 10 MIN.

1 (7-oz.) jar roasted red bell peppers, drained
2 large garlic cloves, chopped
1 cup nonfat yogurt
1 tsp. salt

1. Pulse all ingredients in a blender 5 to 6 times or until smooth.

Linguine With White Clam Sauce

MAKES 4 SERVINGS
PREP: 10 MIN., COOK: 10 MIN.

8 oz. linguine
3 garlic cloves, minced
2 Tbsp. olive oil
1 (8-oz.) bottle clam juice
½ tsp. dried crushed red pepper
3 (6.5-oz.) cans chopped clams, drained
½ cup dry white wine
½ cup chopped fresh parsley
¼ cup chopped fresh basil
2 tsp. fresh lemon juice
1 Tbsp. butter or margarine (optional)

1. Prepare linguine according to package directions; drain and keep warm.
2. Sauté minced garlic in hot oil in a large skillet over medium-high heat 1 to 2 minutes. Add clam juice and dried crushed red pepper; bring to a boil, reduce heat, and simmer 5 minutes. Stir in clams, white wine, and next 3 ingredients; simmer 3 minutes. Toss with warm pasta and, if desired, 1 Tbsp. butter. Serve immediately.

Lime-Peanut Dressing

MAKES 1 CUP
PREP: 10 MIN.

Serve this dressing on salads or with fresh vegetables. You can also toss it with cooked pasta or use it to baste chicken or pork. Fish sauce can be found on the ethnic foods aisle of the grocery store.

½ cup lime juice
3 Tbsp. sugar
2 Tbsp. finely chopped unsalted roasted peanuts
2 Tbsp. fish sauce
1 Tbsp. minced fresh ginger
1 Tbsp. chopped fresh cilantro
4 garlic cloves, minced

1. Stir together all ingredients until blended.

Zucchini-Parmesan Toss

MAKES 4 SERVINGS
PREP: 10 MIN., COOK: 5 MIN.

2 lb. zucchini, cut into ¼-inch-thick slices
2 Tbsp. olive oil
6 Tbsp. freshly grated Parmesan cheese
½ tsp. grated lemon rind
½ tsp. salt
½ tsp. pepper

1. Sauté zucchini in hot oil in a large skillet over medium-high heat 5 minutes or until crisp-tender. Spoon into a serving dish.
2. Combine cheese and next 3 ingredients; reserve 2 Tbsp. cheese mixture. Sprinkle remaining cheese mixture over squash; toss gently. Sprinkle reserved cheese mixture over top. Serve immediately.

Biscuit Poppers
MAKES 2 DOZEN
PREP: 10 MIN., BAKE: 20 MIN.

1 (8-oz.) carton sour cream
½ cup butter, melted
2¼ cups biscuit mix

1. Whisk together sour cream and butter until smooth. Stir in biscuit mix just until moistened. With floured hands, roll into 1½-inch balls. Place in lightly greased mini-muffin cups.
2. Bake at 350° for 18 to 20 minutes or until biscuits are golden brown.

Biscuit Poppers

cook 3 minutes. Add beef broth; bring to a boil, and cook 5 minutes.
2. Stir together ¼ cup water, 2 Tbsp. cornstarch, and ¼ tsp. salt; add to broth mixture, stirring constantly, 1 minute or until mixture thickens to desired consistency. Remove from heat, and serve over pork tenderloins.

Green Beans
MAKES 8 SERVINGS
PREP: 15 MIN., COOK: 10 MIN.

2 lb. fresh green beans, trimmed
½ tsp. salt
¼ cup butter
½ medium-size red bell pepper, sliced
¼ cup chopped pecans (optional)
¼ tsp. pepper

1. Cook green beans with ½ tsp. salt in boiling water to cover in a Dutch oven 6 minutes or until crisp-tender; drain. Plunge into ice water to stop the cooking process; drain again. Pat dry with paper towels.
2. Melt butter in a large skillet over medium heat; add bell pepper and, if desired, pecans, and sauté until butter is lightly browned. Stir in green beans and pepper; cook until thoroughly heated.

Molasses Pork Tenderloin With Red Wine Sauce
MAKES 6 TO 8 SERVINGS
PREP: 10 MIN., CHILL: 8 HRS., GRILL: 20 MIN., STAND: 10 MIN.

make ahead

¾ cup lite soy sauce
1 cup molasses
3 Tbsp. fresh lemon juice
3 Tbsp. olive oil
2 Tbsp. minced fresh ginger
1 large garlic clove, minced
1 (2- to 2½-lb.) package pork tenderloins
Red Wine Sauce

1. Combine first 6 ingredients in a shallow dish or zip-top plastic freezer bag; add tenderloins. Cover or seal, and chill 8 hours. Remove tenderloins from marinade, discarding marinade.
2. Grill tenderloins, covered with grill lid, over medium-high heat (350° to

400°) 20 minutes or until a meat thermometer inserted in thickest portion registers 155°, turning occasionally. Let stand 10 minutes before slicing. Serve with Red Wine Sauce.
Note: Pork tenderloins may be pan-seared in a hot skillet to brown and then baked at 375° for 15 to 20 minutes.
Red Wine Sauce:
MAKES 1¼ CUPS
PREP: 10 MIN., COOK: 12 MIN.

½ small sweet onion, minced
2 Tbsp. butter
½ cup dry red wine
1 (14-oz.) can beef broth
¼ cup water
2 Tbsp. cornstarch
¼ tsp. salt

1. Sauté onion in butter in a large saucepan over medium-high heat 3 minutes or until browned. Add wine, and

Baby Spinach With Pine Nuts
MAKES 4 SERVINGS
PREP: 5 MIN., COOK: 5 MIN.
See page 38 for a suggested menu pairing with Savory Pot Roast and Cheese-Garlic Biscuits (page 27).

2 (6-oz.) packages fresh baby spinach
2 garlic cloves, minced
1 tsp. olive oil
¼ tsp. salt
¼ tsp. pepper
2 Tbsp. toasted pine nuts*

1. Sauté spinach and garlic in hot oil in a large nonstick skillet over medium-high heat 5 minutes or until spinach wilts. Stir in salt and pepper; sprinkle with pine nuts. Serve immediately.
*2 Tbsp. toasted chopped pecans or toasted sliced almonds may be substituted. ▶

Easy Spinach

Crunchy Vegetables

MAKES 4 SERVINGS
PREP: 15 MIN.

Hot chili-sesame oil can be found on the ethnic foods aisle of the grocery store.

1 Tbsp. lime juice
1 tsp. hot chili-sesame oil
1 tsp. sugar
2 small zucchini, cut into thin strips
1 large carrot, cut into thin strips
1 yellow squash, cut into thin strips
¼ tsp. freshly ground pepper

1. Whisk together first 3 ingredients in a large bowl. Add zucchini, carrot, and squash, tossing to coat. Sprinkle evenly with pepper.

Smoked Pork Chops With Jalapeño-Cherry Sauce

MAKES 6 SERVINGS
PREP: 10 MIN., GRILL: 12 MIN.,
COOK: 5 MIN.

6 (1-inch-thick) boneless smoked pork chops
1 (14-oz.) can dark, sweet pitted cherries
1 cup jalapeño jelly
½ tsp. ground coriander

1. Grill pork chops, covered with grill lid, over medium-high heat (350° to 400°) 5 to 6 minutes on each side or until done. Transfer to a serving dish.
2. Bring cherries, jelly, and coriander to a boil in a saucepan, stirring constantly. Pour evenly over pork chops.

Tuna Steaks With Lemon Butter

MAKES 4 SERVINGS
PREP: 10 MIN., COOK: 10 MIN.

¼ cup butter or margarine, softened
2 tsp. lemon juice
4 (1-inch-thick) tuna steaks
½ tsp. salt
½ tsp. freshly ground pepper
2 Tbsp. olive oil

1. Stir together butter and lemon juice.
2. Sprinkle tuna steaks evenly with salt and pepper.

Sautéed Peppers

MAKES 4 SERVINGS
PREP: 15 MIN., COOK: 4 MIN.

1 large red bell pepper
1 large yellow bell pepper
1 large green bell pepper
1 garlic clove, minced
1 Tbsp. olive oil
2 Tbsp. chopped fresh basil
1 tsp. sugar
2 tsp. balsamic vinegar
½ tsp. pepper
¼ tsp. salt

1. Cut peppers into ½-inch strips.
2. Sauté pepper strips and minced garlic in hot oil in a large skillet over medium-high heat 4 minutes or until tender. Stir in chopped basil and remaining ingredients, tossing to coat. Serve immediately.

Easy Spinach

MAKES 4 SERVINGS
PREP: 5 MIN., COOK: 12 MIN.

2 (10-oz.) packages frozen chopped spinach, thawed and well drained
1 garlic clove, chopped
2 Tbsp. olive oil
¼ cup Italian-seasoned breadcrumbs
¼ cup freshly grated Romano cheese
½ tsp. salt
½ tsp. pepper

1. Sauté spinach and garlic in hot oil in a large skillet over medium-high heat 10 to 12 minutes or until thoroughly heated and liquid evaporates. Add breadcrumbs and remaining ingredients, stirring well. Serve immediately.

3. Cook tuna in hot oil in a large non-stick skillet over medium-high heat 5 minutes on each side or until done. Serve immediately with butter mixture.

Sesame Broccoli

MAKES 4 SERVINGS
PREP: 10 MIN., COOK: 12 MIN.

1 lb. fresh broccoli
1 Tbsp. sugar
1 Tbsp. soy sauce
1 Tbsp. vegetable oil
2 tsp. vinegar
2 tsp. toasted sesame seeds

1. Cut broccoli into spears; arrange in a steamer basket over boiling water. Cover and steam 5 minutes or until crisp-tender. Place on a serving platter.
2. Stir together sugar and next 3 ingredients in a small saucepan over medium heat. Cook, stirring often, until sugar dissolves and mixture is thoroughly heated. Drizzle over broccoli, and sprinkle with sesame seeds.

Cream of Pimiento Soup

MAKES 8 CUPS
PREP: 10 MIN.,
COOK: 20 MIN.

make ahead

This recipe easily doubles to serve a crowd.

2 (4-oz.) jars diced pimiento, undrained
¼ cup butter or margarine
⅓ cup all-purpose flour
2 (14-oz.) cans chicken broth
3 cups half-and-half
1 Tbsp. grated onion
1 tsp. salt
½ tsp. hot sauce

1. Process pimiento in a blender or food processor until smooth, stopping to scrape down sides; set aside.
2. Melt ¼ cup butter in a heavy saucepan over low heat; add ⅓ cup flour, and stir until mixture is smooth. Cook, stirring constantly, 1 minute. Add chicken broth and half-and-half gradually to flour mixture; cook over medium heat,

stirring constantly, until mixture is thickened and bubbly.
3. Stir in reserved pimiento, onion, salt, and hot sauce; cook over low heat, stirring constantly, until thoroughly heated.
To Make Ahead: Cover and chill 8 hours. Cook soup over medium heat 8 to 10 minutes or until thoroughly heated. ◆

5-minute sauces

Stir together these sauces to dress up fried chicken strips or steamed shrimp you've picked up on the way home.

■ **Honey Mustard:** Stir together 1 cup mayonnaise, 3 Tbsp. Creole mustard, and 2 Tbsp. honey. Makes about 1¼ cups. Prep: 5 min.

■ **Simple Creole Sauce:** Stir together 1½ cups mayonnaise, 3 Tbsp. Creole mustard, and 1 finely chopped green onion. Makes about 1⅔ cups. Prep: 5 min.

■ **Horseradish Sauce:** Stir together 1 cup mayonnaise, 1 Tbsp. creamy horseradish sauce, and 1 Tbsp. Creole mustard. Makes about 1 cup. Prep: 5 min.

Sesame Broccoli

PHOTOGRAPHS: TINA CORNETT, BETH DREILING, JOHN O'HAGAN, CHARLES WALTON IV / STYLING: BUFFY HARGETT, MINDI SHAPIRO LEVINE, ROSE NGUYEN, CARI SOUTH / FOOD STYLING: PAM LOLLEY, ANGELA SELLERS

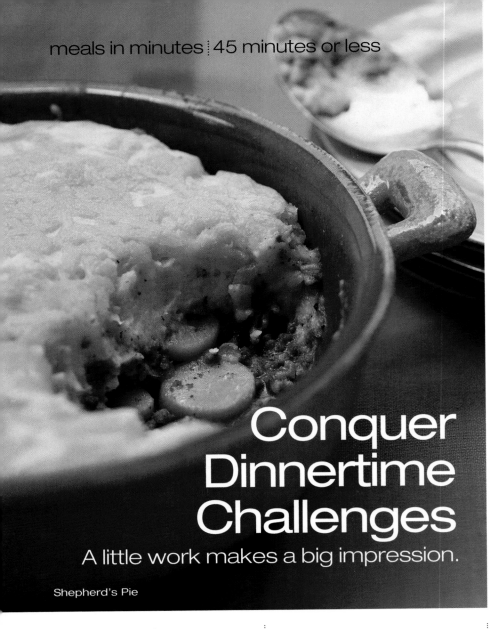

Conquer Dinnertime Challenges

A little work makes a big impression.

Shepherd's Pie

These sure-to-please supper solutions make everyday cooking easier. Several recipes reflect our favorite comfort foods, while others encourage you to try something new.

Shepherd's Pie

MAKES 6 SERVINGS
PREP: 15 MIN., BAKE: 30 MIN.

1 (22-oz.) package frozen mashed potatoes
1 lb. ground beef
1 onion, chopped
½ cup frozen sliced carrots, thawed
2 Tbsp. all-purpose flour
2 tsp. salt, divided
½ tsp. pepper, divided
1 cup beef broth
1 large egg, lightly beaten
½ cup (2 oz.) shredded Cheddar cheese

1. Prepare potatoes according to package directions; set aside.
2. Meanwhile, brown beef and onion in a large skillet over medium-high heat 5 to 6 minutes, stirring until beef crumbles and is no longer pink. Drain and return to skillet; add carrot. Stir in flour, 1 tsp. salt, and ¼ tsp. pepper. Add broth, and cook, stirring constantly, 3 minutes or until slightly thickened. Spoon beef mixture into a lightly greased 11- x 7-inch baking dish.
3. Stir together potatoes, egg, remaining 1 tsp. salt, and remaining ¼ tsp. pepper. Spread evenly over beef mixture.
4. Bake at 350° for 25 minutes. Sprinkle with cheese, and bake 5 more minutes.
Note: For testing purposes, we used Ore-Ida Frozen Mashed Potatoes.

Easy Enchilada Casserole

MAKES 8 SERVINGS
PREP: 15 MIN., COOK: 10 MIN.,
BAKE: 20 MIN.

1 medium onion, chopped
2 Tbsp. vegetable oil
1 (19-oz.) can enchilada sauce
1 (15-oz.) can black beans, rinsed and drained
1 (14½-oz.) can diced tomatoes with green chiles
1 (8-oz.) can Mexican-style corn, drained
1 tsp. fajita seasoning or chili powder
1 tsp. ground cumin
1 (10-oz.) package 6-inch corn tortillas
3 cups chopped cooked chicken*
3 cups (12 oz.) shredded Mexican four-cheese blend

1. Sauté onion in hot oil in a large skillet over medium-high heat until tender. Stir in next 6 ingredients. Reduce heat to low, and cook, stirring often, 5 minutes or until thoroughly heated.
2. Spoon one-third of sauce mixture in bottom of a lightly greased 13- x 9-inch baking dish. Layer with one-third of tortillas, half of chicken, and 1 cup cheese. Repeat layers with one-third each of sauce mixture and tortillas, remaining chicken, and 1 cup cheese. Top with remaining sauce mixture, tortillas, and 1 cup cheese.
3. Bake at 350° for 15 to 20 minutes or until golden and bubbly.
*2 lb. lean ground beef, cooked and drained, may be substituted.

Taco Dinner Mac and Cheese

MAKES 4 SERVINGS
PREP: 15 MIN., COOK: 25 MIN.

8 oz. elbow macaroni
1 lb. ground beef
1 (1.25-oz.) envelope reduced-
    sodium taco seasoning mix
¾ cup water
2 Tbsp. butter
2 Tbsp. all-purpose flour
2 cups milk
1 (8-oz.) block sharp Cheddar
    cheese, shredded
Toppings: chopped tomato,
    chopped avocado, sliced green
    onions, sour cream, salsa

1. Prepare pasta according to package directions. Drain and keep warm.
2. Brown ground beef in a nonstick skillet over medium-high heat until no longer pink. Drain.
3. Return beef to skillet; stir in taco seasoning mix and ¾ cup water. Bring mixture to a boil, and cook, stirring occasionally, 7 minutes or until most of the liquid evaporates. Remove beef mixture from heat.
4. Melt butter in a large saucepan or Dutch oven over medium-low heat; whisk in flour until smooth. Cook, whisking constantly, 2 minutes. Gradually whisk in milk, and cook, whisking constantly, 5 minutes or until thickened. Remove from heat.
5. Stir in 1½ cups Cheddar cheese until melted. Stir in cooked pasta and beef mixture. Sprinkle with remaining ½ cup cheese. Serve immediately with desired toppings.

Steak-and-Spinach Salad With Hot Pan Dressing

MAKES 4 SERVINGS
PREP: 15 MIN., COOK: 20 MIN.
Serve with your favorite crusty garlic bread.

1 (1½-lb.) top sirloin steak
½ tsp. salt
½ tsp. freshly ground pepper
1 tsp. butter, divided
1 tsp. olive oil, divided
2 medium portobello mushroom
    caps, sliced (about 1½ cups)
2 tsp. minced garlic
½ cup red wine
½ cup beef broth
¼ cup balsamic vinegar
1 (6-oz.) package fresh baby spinach
2 plum tomatoes, sliced
1 small red onion, thinly sliced
½ lemon
⅓ cup crumbled Roquefort cheese

1. Sprinkle steak evenly with ½ tsp. salt and ½ tsp. pepper.
2. Heat a large nonstick skillet over medium heat for 2 minutes. Melt ½ tsp. butter with ½ tsp. oil. Add steak, and cook until well browned on 1 side (about 6 minutes). Turn steak, and cook 3 more minutes (rare), 4 minutes (medium-rare), or 5 minutes (medium). Remove steak from pan, and set aside.
3. Melt remaining ½ tsp. butter with ½ tsp. oil in skillet over medium heat. Sauté mushrooms and garlic 4 minutes. Stir in wine, broth, and balsamic vinegar, stirring to loosen particles from bottom of skillet. Bring to a boil; reduce heat, and cook 4 to 5 minutes.
4. Toss together spinach, tomatoes, onion, and hot mushroom mixture in pan; divide evenly among 4 plates. Squeeze lemon juice evenly over top.
5. Cut steak into ½-inch slices, and arrange over salads. Sprinkle cheese evenly over top.

Bacon-Mandarin Salad

MAKES 12 SERVINGS
PREP: 35 MIN.

1 (16-oz.) package bacon
½ cup olive oil
¼ cup red wine vinegar
¼ cup sugar
1 Tbsp. chopped fresh basil
⅛ tsp. hot sauce
2 (11-oz.) cans mandarin oranges,
    drained*
1 head red leaf lettuce, torn
1 head romaine lettuce, torn
1 (4-oz.) package sliced almonds,
    toasted

1. Prepare bacon according to package directions; crumble.
2. Whisk together ½ cup oil and next 4 ingredients in a large bowl, blending well. Add mandarin oranges and lettuces, tossing gently to coat. Sprinkle with crumbled bacon and sliced almonds. Serve immediately.
*Fresh orange segments may be substituted for canned mandarin oranges. ▶

Bacon-Mandarin Salad

Twice-Baked Mashed Potatoes

¼ tsp. ground red pepper
1½ lb. medium-size fresh shrimp, peeled*
1 cup (4 oz.) shredded Monterey Jack cheese
Oyster crackers (optional)

1. Melt butter in a Dutch oven over medium heat; add onion, and sauté 8 minutes or until tender. Stir in cream of potato soup, milk, and pepper; bring to a boil. Add shrimp; reduce heat, and simmer, stirring often, 5 minutes or just until shrimp turn pink. Stir in Monterey Jack cheese until melted. Serve immediately. Serve with oyster crackers, if desired.
*1½ lb. frozen shrimp, thawed; 1½ lb. peeled crawfish tails; or 3 cups chopped cooked chicken may be substituted.

Flank Steak With Tomato-Olive Relish
MAKES 6 SERVINGS
PREP: 10 MIN., COOK: 27 MIN.
Flank steak is generally cooked to medium-rare so it stays tender and juicy. Serve with garlic grits or mashed potatoes.

1½ lb. flank steak
¾ tsp. salt
¾ tsp. coarsely ground pepper
3 Tbsp. olive oil
2 garlic cloves, thinly sliced
½ cup red wine or chicken broth
1 (14½-oz.) can Italian-style diced tomatoes
½ cup pitted black olives, sliced
1 Tbsp. balsamic vinegar
3 Tbsp. minced fresh parsley

1. Sprinkle flank steak evenly with salt and pepper.
2. Cook steak in hot oil in a large skillet over medium-high heat 6 to 8 minutes on each side or to desired degree of doneness.
3. Drain, reserving 1 Tbsp. drippings in skillet; add garlic, and sauté 1 minute. Add wine, tomatoes, olives, and vinegar; cook 10 minutes or until reduced by half. Stir in parsley. Cut steak diagonally across the grain into thin slices; serve with tomato mixture.

Twice-Baked Mashed Potatoes
MAKES 6 SERVINGS
PREP: 15 MIN., BAKE: 20 MIN.
These potatoes are just as delicious when you substitute reduced-fat dairy products. They can also be served family style in a 2-qt. baking dish.

1 (22-oz.) package frozen mashed potatoes
½ (8-oz.) package cream cheese, softened
½ cup sour cream
¼ cup chopped fresh chives
4 bacon slices, cooked and crumbled
½ tsp. seasoned pepper
¼ tsp. salt
½ cup (2 oz.) shredded Cheddar cheese

1. Prepare potatoes according to package directions.
2. Stir in cream cheese and next 5 ingredients. Divide mixture evenly among 6 (6-oz.) lightly greased ramekins or custard cups. Sprinkle evenly with Cheddar cheese.
3. Bake at 350° for 20 minutes or until thoroughly heated.
Note: For testing purposes only, we used Ore-Ida Frozen Mashed Potatoes.

Quick Shrimp Chowder
MAKES 12 CUPS
PREP: 15 MIN., COOK: 20 MIN.
We've streamlined this favorite dish by using canned soup as the base.

2 Tbsp. butter
1 medium onion, chopped
2 (10¾-oz.) cans cream of potato soup
3½ cups milk

Fiesta Turkey Soup With Green Chile Biscuits

MAKES 8 SERVINGS
PREP: 15 MIN., COOK: 30 MIN.

Preheat the oven when you begin. Once the soup is simmering, start the biscuits.

1 medium onion, diced
1 tsp. vegetable oil
1 garlic clove, minced
3 cups chopped cooked turkey or chicken
1 (15-oz.) can chili beans
3½ cups chicken or turkey broth
1 (11-oz.) can yellow corn with red and green bell peppers, drained
1 (10-oz.) can diced tomatoes and green chiles
½ tsp. chili powder
½ tsp. ground cumin
⅛ tsp. salt
⅛ tsp. pepper
Toppings: sour cream, shredded Mexican four-cheese blend
Green Chile Biscuits

1. Sauté onion in hot oil in a large Dutch oven over medium heat 7 minutes or until tender. Add garlic, and sauté 1 minute. Stir in turkey and next 8 ingredients. Bring to a boil, stirring occasionally; reduce heat, and simmer 15 minutes. Serve with desired toppings and Green Chile Biscuits.

Green Chile Biscuits:

MAKES 1 DOZEN
PREP: 5 MIN., BAKE: 12 MIN.

2 cups all-purpose baking mix
1 cup (4 oz.) shredded Mexican four-cheese blend
1 (4.5-oz.) can chopped green chiles, drained
⅔ cup milk

1. Stir together baking mix and remaining ingredients until a soft dough forms. Turn dough out onto a lightly floured surface; knead 3 or 4 times.
2. Pat or roll dough to a ½-inch thickness; cut biscuits with a 2½-inch round cutter, and place on an ungreased baking sheet.
3. Bake at 450° for 10 to 12 minutes or until biscuits are golden brown.
Note: For testing purposes only, we used Bisquick all-purpose baking mix.

Tortilla Soup

MAKES 6 CUPS
PREP: 15 MIN., COOK: 25 MIN.

2 (14-oz.) cans chicken broth
1 (14½-oz.) can Cajun-style stewed tomatoes
3 Tbsp. fresh lemon juice
3 garlic cloves, pressed
2 tsp. chili powder
½ tsp. ground cumin
¼ tsp. ground red pepper
1½ cups chopped cooked chicken
1 cup frozen corn kernels
1 (15-oz.) can black beans, rinsed and drained
2 Tbsp. half-and-half
1 green onion, thinly sliced
Tortilla chips
Toppings: shredded Mexican four-cheese blend, sliced green onions

1. Bring chicken broth and next 6 ingredients to a boil. Reduce heat; add chicken and next 4 ingredients, and simmer 20 minutes. Serve with tortilla chips and desired toppings. ▶

Fiesta Turkey Soup With Green Chile Biscuits

Green Beans With Garlic-Herb Butter

PHOTOGRAPHS:, TINA CORNETT, BETH DREILING, JOHN O'HAGAN, CHARLES WALTON IV / STYLING: MINDI SHAPIRO LEVINE, ROSE NGUYEN, CARI SOUTH / FOOD STYLING: PAM LOLLEY, ANGELA SELLERS

Green Beans With Garlic-Herb Butter

MAKES 4 SERVINGS
PREP: 10 MIN., COOK: 26 MIN.

1 lb. fresh green beans, trimmed
¼ cup butter or margarine
1 small onion, minced
1 celery rib, minced
1½ tsp. bottled minced garlic
¼ tsp. chopped fresh or dried rosemary
¾ tsp. salt
¼ cup chopped fresh parsley

1. Bring salted water to a boil in a large saucepan; add beans, cover, and cook 10 to 15 minutes or until crisp-tender. Drain. Plunge into ice water to stop the cooking process; drain.
2. Melt ¼ cup butter in a saucepan over medium-high heat; add onion and celery, and sauté 5 minutes. Add garlic, and sauté 2 minutes. Stir in beans, rosemary, salt, and parsley; sauté 4 minutes or until thoroughly heated.

Sautéed Green Beans With Bacon

MAKES 4 TO 6 SERVINGS
PREP: 25 MIN., COOK: 15 MIN.

1¾ lb. fresh green beans, trimmed
¼ cup water
8 bacon slices, chopped
5 green onions (white bottoms and light green parts of tops only), chopped
½ tsp. salt
½ tsp. pepper

1. Place beans and ¼ cup water in a large microwave-safe bowl. Cover with plastic wrap, and pierce plastic wrap with a fork. Microwave at HIGH 4 to 7 minutes or until beans are crisp-tender. Plunge green beans into ice water to stop the cooking process. Drain well, and set aside.
2. Cook chopped bacon in a large non-stick skillet over medium heat until crisp; remove bacon, and drain on paper towels, reserving 2 Tbsp. drippings in a small bowl. Discard remaining drippings. Wipe skillet clean with a paper towel.
3. Sauté green onions in skillet in hot reserved drippings over medium-high heat 1 minute. Stir in green beans, salt, and pepper; sauté 2 to 3 minutes or until thoroughly heated. Stir in bacon.
Kitchen Express: Substitute 2 (12-oz.) packages ready-to-eat trimmed

fresh green beans for the fresh green beans, omitting water. Pierce bags with a fork, and microwave at HIGH 4 to 5 minutes or until crisp-tender. Proceed with recipe as directed.

Italian Burgers With Fresh Basil

MAKES 4 SERVINGS
PREP: 20 MIN., GRILL: 18 MIN.

1 lb. lean ground beef
1 small onion, minced
¾ cup grated Parmesan cheese
¼ cup minced fresh parsley
1 large egg, lightly beaten
2 Tbsp. dried Italian seasoning
¾ tsp. pepper
½ tsp. garlic salt
¼ tsp. fennel seeds
4 (1-oz.) provolone cheese slices
4 English muffins, split
½ cup jarred pasta sauce
4 fresh basil sprigs

1. Combine first 9 ingredients; shape into 4 patties.
2. Grill, covered with grill lid, over medium-high heat (350° to 400°) 7 to 8 minutes on each side or until beef is no longer pink. Top patties with cheese, and grill 1 more minute or until cheese melts. Place muffins on grill, cut sides down, and grill 1 minute or until lightly toasted.

3. Top each muffin bottom with 2 Tbsp. pasta sauce, a hamburger patty, a basil sprig, and a muffin top.

Sausage Supper

MAKES 6 SERVINGS
PREP: 20 MIN., COOK: 15 MIN.

1 (16-oz.) package farfalle pasta
1 (19-oz.) package Italian sausage
1 large green bell pepper, chopped
1 large sweet onion, chopped
2 garlic cloves, minced
1 (14-oz.) jar pasta sauce
1 (8-oz.) container soft cream cheese spread
¼ cup sun-dried tomatoes, cut into thin strips
2 tsp. dried Italian seasoning
1 Tbsp. balsamic vinegar (optional)

1. Prepare pasta according to package directions. Drain and keep warm.
2. Remove casings from sausage, and discard. Brown sausage, bell pepper, onion, and garlic in a large skillet over medium-high heat, stirring until sausage crumbles and is no longer pink and vegetables are tender. Drain.
3. Stir in pasta sauce, next 3 ingredients, and, if desired, vinegar. Cook, stirring often, until cream cheese melts and mixture is thoroughly heated. Serve over warm pasta.

Cabbage With Garlic

MAKES 4 TO 5 SERVINGS
PREP: 5 MIN., COOK: 10 MIN.,
BAKE: 25 MIN.

1 small cabbage (about 2 lb.)
6 garlic cloves, finely sliced
3 Tbsp. olive oil
½ cup chicken broth
1 tsp. coarse or kosher salt
Freshly ground pepper to taste

1. Remove and discard outside leaves and stalk from cabbage; cut cabbage into 4 wedges.
2. Sauté garlic in hot oil in an oven-proof skillet over medium heat 1 to 2 minutes or until golden. Add cabbage to skillet, cut sides down; cook 5 minutes. Turn to other cut sides, and cook 2 to 3 minutes. Stir in broth, and sprinkle evenly with salt.
3. Bake at 350° for 20 to 25 minutes or until crisp-tender. Sprinkle evenly with pepper to taste. Serve immediately.

Herb-Roasted Chicken Thighs

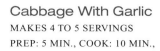

MAKES 4 SERVINGS
PREP: 15 MIN., CHILL: 8 HRS.,
BROIL: 5 MIN., BAKE: 25 MIN.

⅓ cup dry white wine
2 Tbsp. chopped fresh chives
1 Tbsp. chopped fresh parsley
1 garlic clove, minced
2 Tbsp. fresh lemon juice
2 Tbsp. olive oil
2 tsp. Greek seasoning or herbes de Provence
½ tsp. salt
½ tsp. pepper
8 skinned and boned chicken thighs

1. Combine first 9 ingredients in a shallow dish or large heavy-duty zip-top plastic bag; add chicken. Cover or seal, and chill 8 hours.
2. Remove chicken from marinade, discarding marinade. Place chicken on a lightly greased rack in an aluminum foil-lined broiler pan.
3. Broil chicken 5 inches from heat 5 minutes; reduce temperature to 400°, and bake 25 more minutes or until chicken is done.   ◆

Italian Burgers With Fresh Basil

Flavorful Inspiration

Sometimes you have more time to spend cooking. Try one of these terrific options.

Santa Fe Chicken and Dressing

Cooks are always searching for recipes that deliver on flavor, and these do just that. While the ingredient lists may be a little longer, or the prep work more involved, the end results are well worth your efforts.

Santa Fe Chicken and Dressing
MAKES 4 TO 6 SERVINGS
PREP: 15 MIN., BAKE: 40 MIN.

4 cups cubed country-style stuffing
2 cups chopped cooked chicken
1 (15½-oz.) can golden hominy, drained
1 (4.5-oz.) can chopped green chiles, drained
½ cup chopped red bell pepper
½ cup minced fresh cilantro
1 (10¾-oz.) can cream of mushroom soup
1 (8¾-oz.) can cream-style corn
1 cup sour cream
2 tsp. ground cumin
1 cup (4 oz.) shredded Monterey Jack cheese
Tortilla chips (optional)
Salsa (optional)

1. Combine first 6 ingredients in a large bowl; add soup and next 3 ingredients, stirring well. Spread in a lightly greased 2-qt. shallow baking dish.

2. Bake, covered, at 350° for 35 minutes or until thoroughly heated. Uncover and sprinkle evenly with cheese; bake 5 more minutes or until cheese melts. Serve with tortilla chips and salsa, if desired.

Shrimp Oriental
MAKES 4 SERVINGS
PREP: 40 MIN., COOK: 10 MIN.

2 lb. unpeeled, large fresh shrimp
2 (8-oz.) cans pineapple chunks, undrained
½ cup sugar
2 Tbsp. cornstarch
1 tsp. salt
¼ cup rice wine vinegar
2 Tbsp. chili sauce
⅓ cup ketchup
1 tsp. soy sauce
1 green bell pepper, diced
1 red bell pepper, diced
Hot cooked rice (optional)

1. Peel shrimp, and devein, if desired. Set shrimp aside.

2. Drain pineapple, reserving juice. Stir together pineapple juice, sugar, and next 6 ingredients.

3. Cook pineapple juice mixture in a large skillet or wok over high heat, stirring constantly, 15 to 30 seconds or until thickened. Add diced bell peppers, and cook 3 to 4 minutes. Add pineapple chunks and shrimp. Cook, stirring often, 3 to 5 minutes or just until shrimp turn pink. Serve over hot cooked rice, if desired.

Chicken Oriental: Substitute 4 skinned and boned chicken breast halves, cubed, for shrimp. Cook for 10 minutes or until chicken is done.

Hoisin Chicken-and-Pasta Salad

MAKES 6 SERVINGS
PREP: 30 MIN., COOK: 20 MIN.

16 oz. penne pasta
½ cup vegetable oil, divided
1 garlic clove, pressed
4 skinned and boned chicken
    breast halves
½ cup chicken broth
½ cup Hoisin Mixture
2 celery ribs, sliced
2 green onions, sliced
1 small cucumber, peeled, seeded,
    and sliced
½ small red bell pepper, cut into
    thin strips
¾ tsp. salt
¾ tsp. pepper
Mixed salad greens
2 tsp. toasted sesame seeds

1. Prepare pasta according to package directions. Drain. Return to Dutch oven, and toss with 3 Tbsp. oil.
2. Heat remaining 5 Tbsp. oil in a large skillet over medium heat; add garlic, and sauté 1 minute. Add chicken, and cook 4 minutes on each side or until done. Remove chicken from skillet. Stir in chicken broth; bring to a boil. Reduce heat, and simmer 10 minutes or until reduced to ⅓ cup; remove from heat, and stir in Hoisin Mixture. Toss with pasta.
3. Cut chicken into ½-inch cubes. Add chicken, celery, and next 5 ingredients to pasta mixture; toss well. Spoon over salad greens; sprinkle with sesame seeds. Serve immediately.

Hoisin Mixture:

MAKES 1¼ CUPS
PREP: 5 MIN.
This mixture also adds great flavor to stir-fry vegetables.

1 (7.25-oz.) jar hoisin sauce
1½ Tbsp. sugar
2 Tbsp. pale dry sherry
1½ Tbsp. rice vinegar

1. Stir together all ingredients until sugar dissolves. Store in refrigerator up to 3 months.
Note: Hoisin sauce may be found on the ethnic foods aisle of the grocery store.

Sweet-and-Spicy Pork

MAKES 4 SERVINGS
PREP: 10 MIN., BAKE: 30 MIN.,
STAND: 10 MIN.

4 garlic cloves, minced
1 Tbsp. hoisin sauce
1 Tbsp. Dijon mustard
1 Tbsp. ketchup
2 Tbsp. lite soy sauce, divided
6 tsp. honey, divided
1 (¾-lb.) pork tenderloin
2 tsp. rice vinegar
1 tsp. sesame oil
1 tsp. Asian garlic-chili sauce
½ cup chopped green onions
¼ cup chopped fresh cilantro

1. Stir together minced garlic, next 3 ingredients, 1 Tbsp. soy sauce, and 2 tsp. honey.
2. Spoon garlic mixture evenly over pork, rubbing well into meat. Place pork on a lightly greased rack in an aluminum foil-lined roasting pan.
3. Bake at 350° for 30 minutes or until a meat thermometer inserted in thickest portion of tenderloin registers 155°. Remove from oven; cover pork loosely with aluminum foil, and let stand 10 minutes. Cut pork diagonally into slices, and place slices on a serving platter.
4. Whisk together rice vinegar, sesame oil, Asian garlic-chili sauce, remaining 1 Tbsp. soy sauce, and remaining 4 tsp. honey. Drizzle evenly over pork. Sprinkle evenly with chopped green onions and cilantro. ▶

Hoisin Chicken-and-Pasta Salad

PHOTOGRAPHS: RALPH ANDERSON, BETH DREILING, JOHN O'HAGAN / STYLING: MINDI SHAPIRO LEVINE, ROSE NGUYEN / FOOD STYLING: PAM LOLLEY, ANGELA SELLERS

Eye of Round Roast
and Roasted Potatoes

Eye of Round Roast

MAKES 4 SERVINGS

PREP: 15 MIN., CHILL: 8 HRS.,
STAND: 30 MIN., BAKE: 1 HR.

make ahead

The time listed reads longer than 60 minutes, but this make-ahead recipe really saves you time. You prep the meat, cover and chill 8 hours or overnight, and then bake. A little work in advance delivers lots of flavor.

1 (2.5-lb.) eye of round roast
1 (5-oz.) jar Chinese sweet-hot
    mustard
3 Tbsp. olive oil
2 garlic cloves, pressed
2 tsp. lite soy sauce
1 tsp. Worcestershire sauce
Roasted Potatoes, uncooked

1. Place roast on an 18- x 11-inch piece of heavy-duty aluminum foil.
2. Stir together mustard, olive oil, garlic, soy sauce, and Worcestershire sauce; spread over roast. Fold foil over roast to seal. Place in a shallow roasting pan, and chill at least 8 hours. Remove roast from foil; place in roasting pan. Let stand 15 minutes.
3. Bake, covered, at 450° for 20 minutes. Arrange uncooked Roasted Potatoes around roast, and bake, uncovered, 40 more minutes or until potatoes are tender and roast is desired degree of doneness. Remove pan from oven; lightly cover, and let stand 15 minutes before slicing.

Roasted Potatoes:

MAKES 4 SERVINGS

PREP: 10 MIN., BAKE: 25 MIN.

4 medium potatoes, cut into
    8 wedges
2 medium onions, cut into
    wedges
2 Tbsp. olive oil
2 garlic cloves, pressed
1 tsp. salt
½ tsp. pepper

1. Toss together all ingredients.

Teriyaki Meat Loaf

MAKES 4 SERVINGS

PREP: 15 MIN., BAKE: 40 MIN.

make ahead

To make ahead, combine the ingredients, and shape into a loaf the night before. Then let it stand at room temperature while the oven preheats.

⅔ cup orange marmalade
3 Tbsp. teriyaki sauce, divided
2 Tbsp. seasoned rice wine vinegar
¼ tsp. crushed red pepper
1 lb. ground beef
1 cup soft breadcrumbs
½ cup finely chopped roasted
    peanuts
1 Tbsp. fresh lime juice
½ tsp. ground ginger
½ tsp. minced garlic
1 large egg
Hot cooked rice or mashed potatoes

1. Stir together marmalade, 2 Tbsp. teriyaki sauce, vinegar, and red pepper. Set aside.
2. Combine ground beef, next 6 ingredients, and remaining 1 Tbsp. teriyaki sauce. Shape into a 4- x 7- inch loaf. Place in a 9-inch pan or baking dish.
3. Bake at 350° for 30 minutes. Remove from oven, and pour marmalade mixture over meat; bake 8 to 10 more minutes or until done. Serve with hot cooked rice or mashed potatoes, and drizzle with pan juices, if desired.

Easy Beef Casserole

MAKES 4 TO 6 SERVINGS

PREP: 20 MIN., BAKE: 30 MIN.

make ahead

To make ahead, prepare the recipe up to topping with the seasoned potatoes. Cover and chill. Let stand at room temperature while the oven preheats. Top with potatoes; bake.

1 lb. ground beef
¼ tsp. salt
½ (16-oz.) package frozen mixed
    vegetables
1 (10¾-oz.) can cream of chicken
    soup
1 cup (4 oz.) shredded Cheddar
    cheese
½ (32-oz.) package frozen
    seasoned potatoes

1. Cook ground beef and salt in a large skillet over medium heat, stirring until meat crumbles and is no longer pink; drain well. Spoon ground beef into a lightly greased 2½-qt. shallow baking dish.

2. Layer vegetables, soup, and cheese over ground beef. Top with potatoes.

3. Bake at 400° for 30 minutes or until potatoes are golden.

Note: For testing purposes only, we used Ore-Ida Tater Tots.

Pork Skillet Dinner
MAKES 4 SERVINGS
PREP: 10 MIN., COOK: 45 MIN.

---

4 (½-inch-thick) bone-in pork chops
¾ tsp. salt, divided
¼ tsp. pepper
3 Tbsp. all-purpose flour
1 Tbsp. vegetable oil
3 medium-size baking potatoes,
   cut into 1-inch pieces
4 large carrots, cut into
   1-inch-thick slices
1 small onion, chopped
1 celery rib, chopped
1 (14-oz.) can chicken broth

---

1. Sprinkle pork chops with ½ tsp. salt and ¼ tsp. pepper; dredge in flour. Brown pork chops in hot oil in a large skillet over medium heat, and drain. Top with potato pieces and next 3 ingredients; sprinkle with remaining ¼ tsp. salt.

2. Pour broth over vegetables. Cover and cook over medium-low heat 40 minutes or until vegetables are tender and chops are done.

Pork in Garlic Sauce
MAKES 4 SERVINGS
PREP: 25 MIN., STAND: 15 MIN.,
COOK: 9 MIN.

---

4 tsp. cornstarch, divided
5½ Tbsp. soy sauce, divided
1 lb. lean, boneless pork chops,
   cut into thin strips
1 cup uncooked long-grain rice
¼ cup water
4 tsp. hoisin sauce
1 tsp. sesame oil
1 Tbsp. peanut oil
½ (8-oz.) package sliced fresh
   mushrooms
4 green onions, sliced

1 (8-oz.) can sliced water
   chestnuts, drained
3 garlic cloves, minced
2 tsp. minced fresh ginger
½ tsp. dried crushed red pepper
2 Tbsp. fresh orange juice
Garnishes: chopped green onions,
   orange slices

---

1. Stir together 2 tsp. cornstarch and 1½ Tbsp. soy sauce in a medium bowl until smooth. Add pork strips, tossing to coat. Let stand 15 minutes.

2. Prepare rice according to package directions. Keep warm.

3. Stir together remaining 2 tsp. cornstarch, remaining 4 Tbsp. soy sauce, ¼ cup water, and hoisin sauce.

4. Heat sesame and peanut oils in a large skillet or wok over medium-high heat 2 minutes. Add pork mixture, and stir-fry 3 to 4 minutes or until pork is browned. Add sliced mushrooms, green onions, and next 4 ingredients; stir-fry 2 minutes. Stir in hoisin sauce mixture, and stir-fry 1 minute or until thickened. Stir in 2 Tbsp. orange juice. Serve over warm rice, and garnish, if desired. ◆

Pork in Garlic Sauce

Smothered Chicken

MAKES 4 SERVINGS
PREP: 20 MIN., COOK: 40 MIN.

Peel the garlic cloves, and crush them with the heel of your hand on a cutting board. A longer cooking time is needed to soften the larger pieces and mellow the flavor.

4 skinned and boned chicken
  breasts
¾ tsp. salt, divided
½ tsp. pepper, divided
½ cup Italian-seasoned
  breadcrumbs
1 (8-oz.) package sliced fresh
  mushrooms
1 tsp. olive oil
18 to 20 garlic cloves, crushed
2 Tbsp. olive oil, divided
2 Tbsp. butter or margarine, divided
1 (14-oz.) can chicken broth
1 Tbsp. fresh lemon juice
½ tsp. dried basil
¼ tsp. dried oregano
3 Tbsp. all-purpose flour
¼ cup water

1. Place chicken between 2 sheets of heavy-duty plastic wrap; flatten to a ¼-inch thickness, using a meat mallet or rolling pin. Sprinkle both sides of chicken evenly with ½ tsp. salt and ¼ tsp. pep-per. Dredge in breadcrumbs. Set aside.

2. Sauté mushrooms in 1 tsp. hot oil in a large nonstick skillet over medium-high heat 8 minutes or until edges are browned. Remove from skillet. Sprinkle with remaining ¼ tsp. salt and ¼ tsp. pepper; set aside.

3. Sauté garlic in 1 Tbsp. hot oil over medium heat 5 to 10 minutes or until lightly browned and soft. Remove from skillet, and mash lightly with a fork or potato masher; set aside.

4. Melt 1 Tbsp. butter with ½ Tbsp. oil in skillet over medium heat; add 2 chicken breasts, and cook 4 minutes on each side or until done. Remove chicken to a wire rack in a jelly-roll pan. Keep chicken warm in a 225° oven. Repeat with remaining butter, oil, and chicken.

5. Stir chicken broth and next 3 ingredients into skillet, and cook 2 minutes, stirring to loosen particles from bottom of skillet. Stir in sautéed mushrooms and garlic.

6. Stir together 3 Tbsp. flour and ¼ cup water; whisk into broth mixture over medium-high heat. Cook, whisking constantly, 3 minutes or until thickened. ◆

Here's the plan: Start Rice Pilaf, and prepare Sautéed Peppers while the rice cooks. Tuna Steaks With Lemon Butter are ready in just 10 minutes.

Quick To Assemble

All the recipes featured in this chapter have short hands-on times, which means that the recipe either comes together quickly from start to finish or has speedy prep (with the remaining time being hands-off). Discover the magic that a marinade works on less expensive cuts of meat and the benefits of a slow cooker. As a welcome change for the busiest of evenings, choose breakfast foods or hearty knife-and-fork sandwiches.

Breakfast Anytime
Serve the familiar morning meal in the evening instead.

Cooking bacon or sausage, scrambled eggs, and toast for supper is often a last-minute solution at the end of a busy day. It's fast, and you probably have most of the ingredients on hand. Take that thought to the next level, and plan these family favorite selections for your evening meal. Southwest Egg Casserole is great to take to a sick friend, to welcome neighbors, or when a new baby arrives.

Waffles
MAKES 10 (4-INCH) WAFFLES
PREP: 5 MIN., COOK: 15 MIN.

2 cups all-purpose baking mix
½ cup vegetable oil
2 large eggs
1 cup club soda

1. Stir together first 3 ingredients in a large bowl; add club soda, stirring until batter is blended.
2. Cook in a preheated, greased waffle iron until golden.

Cheese-Garlic Biscuits

MAKES 2 DOZEN
PREP: 10 MIN., BAKE: 8 MIN.

4 cups all-purpose baking mix
1⅓ cups milk
1 cup (4 oz.) shredded Cheddar
   cheese
½ cup butter or margarine, melted
1 Tbsp. minced fresh parsley
1 tsp. garlic powder

1. Stir together baking mix, milk, and shredded Cheddar cheese until a soft dough forms.
2. Drop by heaping tablespoonfuls onto a lightly greased baking sheet.
3. Bake at 450° for 6 to 8 minutes or until golden.
4. Stir together melted butter, minced parsley, and garlic powder; brush over warm biscuits.

Southwest Egg Casserole

MAKES 6 TO 8 SERVINGS
PREP: 15 MIN., COOK: 25 MIN.,
BAKE: 30 MIN.

This recipe received our highest rating. You can prepare it the night before and pop it in the oven when you're ready to eat. Let it stand at room temperature 30 minutes before baking.

1 lb. mild ground pork sausage
1 small onion, chopped
½ green bell pepper, chopped
2 (10-oz.) cans diced tomatoes and
   green chiles
8 (10-inch) flour tortillas, torn into
   bite-size pieces
3 cups (12 oz.) shredded colby-
   Jack cheese blend
6 large eggs
2 cups milk
1 tsp. salt
½ tsp. pepper

1. Cook sausage in a large skillet over medium-high heat, stirring until it crumbles and is no longer pink. Drain and return to skillet. Add chopped onion and bell pepper to sausage in skillet; sauté over medium-high heat 5 minutes or until vegetables are tender. Stir in 2 cans tomatoes and green chiles; reduce heat, and simmer 10 minutes.
2. Layer half each of tortilla pieces, sausage mixture, and cheese in a lightly greased 13- x 9-inch baking dish. Repeat layers.
3. Whisk together eggs, milk, salt, and pepper; pour over layers in baking dish. Cover and chill up to 8 hours, if desired.
4. Bake, lightly covered with aluminum foil, at 350° for 30 minutes or until golden and bubbly.

Ham-and-Broccoli Omelet

Ham-and-Broccoli Omelet

MAKES 10 TO 12 SERVINGS
PREP: 15 MIN., BAKE: 30 MIN.

Simplify your meal planning by purchasing diced ham in the deli section of your supermarket.

2 Tbsp. butter
2 cups diced cooked ham
1 medium-size sweet onion, diced
2½ cups chopped fresh broccoli
1 tsp. salt
¾ tsp. freshly ground pepper
12 large eggs
½ cup sour cream
¼ tsp. baking powder
6 plum tomatoes, seeded and
   chopped
1 (8-oz.) block Havarti cheese with
   jalapenos, shredded*
½ cup chopped fresh basil (optional)

1. Melt butter in a 12-inch ovenproof skillet; add ham, onion, and broccoli. Sauté 5 minutes. Stir in salt and pepper.
2. Beat eggs, sour cream, and baking powder at medium speed with an electric mixer 2 to 3 minutes. Pour over ham mixture.
3. Bake at 350° for 15 minutes. Remove from oven, and sprinkle with tomatoes, cheese, and, if desired, basil. Bake 15 more minutes or until set. Serve immediately.
*1 (8-oz.) package shredded sharp Cheddar cheese may be substituted.

Breakfast-Stuffed Potatoes

MAKES 6 SERVINGS
PREP: 20 MIN., COOK: 5 MIN.,
BAKE: 15 MIN.

A blend of cheeses, bacon, onion, and broccoli pack these potatoes with enough flavor to satisfy the heartiest appetites.

6 (4-oz.) Yukon gold potatoes
¼ cup half-and-half
½ (8-oz.) package cream cheese,
   softened
2 Tbsp. grated Parmesan cheese
¼ tsp. garlic salt
¼ tsp. freshly ground pepper
4 bacon slices, cooked and
   crumbled
½ small sweet onion, chopped
½ (10-oz.) package frozen chopped
   broccoli, thawed and drained
¼ cup (1 oz.) shredded Cheddar
   cheese

1. Prick potatoes several times with a fork, and place in microwave; cover with damp paper towels. Microwave at HIGH 8 to 10 minutes or until tender; cool slightly.
2. Cut potatoes in half crosswise; gently scoop out pulp, leaving a ¼-inch-thick shell and reserving pulp. Stand potato shells, cut sides up, in muffin pan cups for stuffing.
3. Stir together reserved pulp, half-and-half, and next 5 ingredients.
4. Sauté onion and thawed broccoli in a nonstick skillet over medium-high heat 4 to 5 minutes or until tender. Stir into potato mixture. Stuff mixture evenly into potato shells. Sprinkle with Cheddar cheese.
5. Bake stuffed potatoes at 350° for 15 minutes. ◆

Knife-and-Fork Sandwiches

Check out these hearty recipes— all stacked up on fresh bread.

These satisfying sandwiches are a big step above their lunchbox cousins. You're gonna need a knife and fork to make sure you don't miss a single sliver of luscious meat or a crumb of bread. If you haven't considered it before, now is the time to try sandwiches for supper.

Easy Meat Loaf Sandwiches

MAKES 4 SERVINGS
PREP: 15 MIN.

½ cup mayonnaise
8 hearty bread slices
4 (½-inch-thick) Easy Meat Loaf slices
Shredded lettuce
1 tomato, sliced
Salt and pepper to taste

1. Spread 1 Tbsp. mayonnaise on 1 side of each bread slice. Top each of 4 bread slices, mayonnaise sides up, with a slice of Easy Meat Loaf, shredded lettuce, and tomato; sprinkle evenly with salt and pepper to taste. Top with remaining bread slices, mayonnaise sides down. .

Easy Meat Loaf:

MAKES 4 SERVINGS
PREP: 10 MIN., BAKE: 45 MIN.

1 lb. lean ground beef
½ cup quick-cooking oats, uncooked
1 Tbsp. instant minced onion
1 Tbsp. dried parsley flakes
1 Tbsp. dried celery flakes
1 tsp. salt
½ tsp. pepper
1 Tbsp. Worcestershire sauce
1 large egg
½ cup milk
4 Tbsp. ketchup

1. Combine first 10 ingredients and 2 Tbsp. ketchup; shape into a loaf, and place in a lightly greased 13- x 9-inch pan. Top with remaining 2 Tbsp. ketchup.
2. Bake at 350° for 45 minutes or until done.

Deli-Stuffed Sandwiches

MAKES 8 SERVINGS
PREP: 10 MIN.

2 Tbsp. olive oil
½ cup chopped ripe olives*
1 Tbsp. chopped fresh or 1 tsp.
   dried oregano
1 Tbsp. cider vinegar
½ tsp. pepper
1 (16-oz.) round Italian bread loaf
¼ lb. thinly sliced cooked turkey
¼ lb. thinly sliced cooked ham
1 (8-oz.) package shredded Italian
   three-cheese blend

1. Stir together first 5 ingredients.
2. Cut bread loaf in half horizontally; remove center of bread, and reserve for other uses, leaving a ½-inch-thick shell.
3. Spoon half of olive mixture into bread shell. Top with turkey, ham, cheese, and remaining olive mixture. Cover with bread top. Cut into wedges. Serve immediately.
*½ cup chopped pimiento-stuffed Spanish olives may be substituted.

Deli-Stuffed Sandwiches

Guacamole-Topped Ham Po'boys

MAKES 6 SERVINGS
PREP: 20 MIN., BROIL: 1 MIN.
This open-faced sandwich is brimming with flavor.

2 medium avocados, halved
½ cup diced tomatoes and green
   chiles
¼ cup sour cream
2 tsp. lemon juice
2 green onions, chopped
1 garlic glove, minced
1 tsp. salt
¼ tsp. pepper
¼ cup mayonnaise
¼ cup Creole mustard
6 French rolls, split
2 lb. deli-sliced ham
12 (¾-oz.) Monterey Jack cheese
   slices
Shredded lettuce
2 medium tomatoes, sliced

1. Scoop avocado pulp into bowl; mash with a fork or potato masher just until chunky. Stir in ½ cup diced tomatoes and green chiles, sour cream, and next 5 ingredients. Set guacamole aside.
2. Spread mayonnaise and mustard evenly over cut sides of rolls; layer each half evenly with ham and cheese. Place on a baking sheet.
3. Broil 2 inches from heat 1 minute or until cheese melts.
4. Top evenly with lettuce, tomato slices, and guacamole.
Note: 1 cup prepared guacamole may be substituted for first 8 ingredients.

Egg Salad Club Sandwiches

MAKES 4 SERVINGS
PREP: 25 MIN.
Substitute fresh arugula for the spinach if you prefer its spicy bite. For a checkerboard effect, you can use both white and wheat breads. If you want to serve only the salad, omit the bread, spinach, and ⅓ cup mayonnaise.

⅔ cup mayonnaise, divided
4 large hard-cooked eggs,
   chopped
1 celery rib, diced
4 bacon slices, cooked and
   crumbled
¼ cup chopped fresh chives
1 Tbsp. minced sweet onion
¼ tsp. seasoned salt
½ tsp. freshly ground pepper
12 very thin white or wheat sandwich
   bread slices, lightly toasted
1 cup firmly packed fresh spinach

1. Stir together ⅓ cup mayonnaise and next 7 ingredients.
2. Spread remaining ⅓ cup mayonnaise evenly over 1 side of 8 bread slices. Spread 4 bread slices, mayonnaise sides up, evenly with half of egg salad. Top evenly with half of spinach and 4 bread slices without mayonnaise. Repeat procedure with remaining egg salad and spinach. Top with remaining bread slices, mayonnaise sides down. Cut each sandwich into quarters.
Sweet Pickle-Egg Salad Club: Omit bacon and chives. Add 2 Tbsp. instant potato flakes and 1 Tbsp. sweet pickle relish; proceed with recipe as directed.
Shrimp-Egg Salad Club: Omit bacon. Add ⅔ cup finely chopped boiled shrimp, ½ tsp. grated lemon rind, and ¼ tsp. ground red pepper. Proceed with recipe as directed. ►

Catfish Sandwiches

Chuck Roast Barbecue Sandwiches

MAKES 6 SERVINGS
PREP: 15 MIN., COOK: 6 HRS.

make ahead

Serve with potato chips and pickle spears, if desired.

1 (2- to 2½-lb.) boneless chuck roast, trimmed
2 medium onions, chopped
¾ cup cola soft drink
¼ cup Worcestershire sauce
1 Tbsp. apple cider vinegar
2 garlic cloves, minced
1 tsp. beef bouillon granules
½ tsp. dry mustard
½ tsp. chili powder
¼ tsp. ground red pepper
½ cup ketchup
2 tsp. butter or margarine
6 hamburger buns

1. Combine roast and onions in a 4-qt. slow cooker.
2. Combine cola and next 7 ingredients; reserve ½ cup mixture in refrigerator. Pour remaining mixture over roast and onions.
3. Cook, covered, on HIGH 6 hours or until roast is very tender; drain and shred roast. Keep warm.
4. Combine reserved ½ cup cola mixture, ketchup, and butter in a small saucepan; cook mixture over medium heat, stirring constantly, just until thoroughly heated. Pour over shredded roast, stirring gently. Spoon onto buns.

Chuck Roast Barbecue Sandwiches

Catfish Sandwiches

MAKES 4 SERVINGS
PREP: 15 MIN., FRY: 10 MIN.

¾ cup yellow cornmeal
¼ cup all-purpose flour
2 tsp. salt
1 tsp. ground red pepper
¼ tsp. garlic powder
4 catfish fillets (about 1½ lb.)
¼ tsp. salt
Vegetable oil
4 onion sandwich buns, split and toasted
Tartar or cocktail sauce
Lettuce leaves
4 tomato slices (optional)

1. Combine first 5 ingredients in a large shallow dish.
2. Sprinkle fish with ¼ tsp. salt; dredge in flour mixture, coating well.
3. Pour oil to a depth of 3 inches in a Dutch oven; heat to 350°. Fry fish 4 to 5 minutes on each side or until golden brown. Drain on paper towels.
4. Serve catfish on sandwich buns with tartar sauce, lettuce, and, if desired, tomato slices.

Hot Chicken Salad Sandwiches

MAKES 6 SERVINGS
PREP: 10 MIN., BROIL: 3 MIN.,
BAKE: 10 MIN.

1 (10-oz.) can chunk white chicken, drained and flaked
1 (8-oz.) can pineapple tidbits, drained
1 cup (4 oz.) shredded Cheddar cheese
¼ cup finely chopped green bell pepper
2 Tbsp. finely chopped celery
1 Tbsp. finely chopped onion
⅓ cup mayonnaise or dressing
1 tsp. salt
3 Kaiser rolls, split

1. Combine chicken, pineapple, Cheddar cheese, and next 5 ingredients, stirring well. Place rolls, cut sides up, on a baking sheet.
2. Broil rolls 5 inches from heat until lightly browned. Spread filling evenly over rolls.
3. Bake at 350° for 5 to 10 minutes or until thoroughly heated.

Reuben Sandwiches

Reuben Sandwiches

MAKES 4 SERVINGS
PREP: 15 MIN., COOK: 8 MIN.

2 cups sauerkraut, drained
½ cup mayonnaise
2 Tbsp. ketchup
2 green onions, chopped
12 thin pumpernickel-rye swirl
    bread slices
1 lb. thinly sliced deli corned beef
8 (1-oz.) Swiss cheese slices

1. Press sauerkraut between paper towels to remove excess moisture.
2. Stir together sauerkraut, mayonnaise, ketchup, and green onions.
3. Top 4 bread slices with half of corned beef, half of sauerkraut mixture, and half of cheese. Repeat layers, and top with remaining bread slices.
4. Cook sandwiches in a large lightly greased skillet or griddle over medium heat 4 minutes on each side. Serve immediately.
Note: For testing purposes only, we used Pepperidge Farm Deli Swirl Bread.

Club Wraps

MAKES 4 SERVINGS
PREP: 25 MIN.

½ cup mustard-mayonnaise blend
4 (10-inch) flour tortillas
½ lb. thinly sliced smoked turkey
½ lb. thinly sliced honey ham
1 cup (4 oz.) shredded smoked
    provolone or mozzarella
    cheese
2 cups shredded leaf lettuce
2 medium tomatoes, seeded and
    chopped
½ small red onion, diced
8 bacon slices, cooked and
    crumbled
½ tsp. salt
½ tsp. pepper

1. Spread mustard-mayonnaise blend evenly over 1 side of each tortilla, leaving a ½-inch border. Layer turkey and next 6 ingredients evenly over tortillas; sprinkle with salt and pepper.
2. Roll up tortillas; secure with wooden picks, and cut in half diagonally.

Grilled Ham-and-Cheese Sandwiches

MAKES 4 SERVINGS
PREP: 10 MIN., COOK: 8 MIN.

2 cups (8 oz.) shredded Cheddar-
    Monterey Jack cheese blend
1 (3-oz.) package cream cheese,
    softened
¼ cup mayonnaise
1 Tbsp. prepared horseradish
2 green onions, diced
8 sandwich bread slices
8 cooked ham slices
4 Tbsp. butter, softened

1. Stir together first 5 ingredients, and spread mixture on 1 side of 4 bread slices. Top each with 2 ham slices and remaining bread slices.
2. Spread half of butter evenly on 1 side of sandwiches. Cook sandwiches, in batches, buttered sides down, in a hot nonstick skillet over medium-high heat 2 minutes or until browned. Spread remaining butter on ungrilled sides; turn and cook 2 minutes or until browned. ◆

quick to assemble

Slow-cooker Recipes

You don't need to be in the kitchen for these meals. They cook themselves.

Easy Spanish Pork Dip Sandwiches

Slow cookers are the must-have time-saving appliances. While they may make you think of mom, today's advanced models are perfect for busy cooks. To start dinner, all you have to do is plug it in that morning, add the ingredients in the correct order, cover, and turn it on. Then you're out the door to work or off to other duties around the house. You'll come back to a tasty, satisfying meal.

Easy Spanish Pork Dip Sandwiches

MAKES 8 SANDWICHES
PREP: 20 MIN., COOK: 6 HRS.

make ahead

Find mojo criollo on the Hispanic foods aisle of your grocery store.

---

3 Tbsp. garlic pepper
2 tsp. salt
1 (4- to 5-lb.) boneless pork shoulder roast, cut in half
¼ cup vegetable oil
¾ cup mojo criollo Spanish marinating sauce
2 (0.87-oz.) envelopes pork gravy mix
2 cups water
¼ cup white vinegar
2 bay leaves
1 medium-size sweet onion, thinly sliced
8 mini French rolls

---

1. Sprinkle garlic pepper and salt evenly over roast. Cook roast in hot oil in a large skillet 2 minutes on each side or until lightly browned. Place in a 6-qt. slow cooker, fat sides up.

2. Combine Spanish marinating sauce and next 3 ingredients; pour over roast in slow cooker. Add bay leaves; top with sliced onion.

3. Cover and cook on HIGH 1 hour. Reduce heat to LOW, and cook 4 to 5 hours or until meat is tender and shreds easily. Remove and discard bay leaves.

4. Remove pork to a large bowl, reserving liquid and onion slices in slow cooker; shred pork with two forks. Add 1 cup reserved liquid to shredded pork to moisten.

5. Slice mini French rolls in half. Place shredded pork and onion slices on bottom bread slices; top with remaining bread slices.

6. Spoon remaining reserved liquid into individual bowls for dipping.

Note: For testing purposes only, we used La Lechonera Mojo Criollo.

Pork roast simmers slowly in marinating sauce.

When the pork is falling-apart tender, remove it from the slow cooker; reserve liquid and onion slices. Shred the meat with 2 forks, and place it in a bowl.

Remove onion slices with a slotted spoon. Skim fat from juices in slow cooker, or pour liquid into a fat strainer; let stand until fat rises to top. Discard fat. Pour 1 cup juices into shredded meat in bowl, tossing to coat. Pour remaining juices into individual bowls for dipping.

To make ahead and freeze: Place meat and 1 cup juices in a large zip-top plastic freezer bag. Place onions and ½ cup juices in a separate bag. Seal and freeze up to one month. Pour remaining juices into a large container; cover and chill eight hours. Remove and discard fat from top. Freeze up to one month.

Potato Soup

MAKES 12 CUPS
PREP: 20 MIN., COOK: 8 HRS.

6 large russet potatoes, peeled and cut into ½-inch cubes (about 3¾ lb.)
1 large onion, chopped (about 1½ cups)
3 (14-oz.) cans seasoned chicken broth with roasted garlic
¼ cup butter
2½ tsp. salt
1¼ tsp. freshly ground pepper
1 cup whipping cream or half-and-half
1 cup (4 oz.) sharp Cheddar cheese, shredded
3 Tbsp. chopped fresh chives
1 (8-oz.) container sour cream (optional)
4 bacon slices, cooked and crumbled
Shredded Cheddar cheese

1. Combine first 6 ingredients in a 5-qt. slow cooker.
2. Cover and cook on HIGH 4 hours or on LOW 8 hours or until potatoes are tender. Mash mixture until potatoes are coarsely chopped and soup is slightly thickened; stir in cream, cheese, and chives. Top with sour cream, if desired, and sprinkle with bacon and Cheddar cheese before serving.

Apple Cider Pork and Vegetables

MAKES 4 SERVINGS
PREP: 15 MIN., COOK: 8 HRS.

4 small sweet potatoes, peeled and cut into ½-inch slices
1 (7-oz.) package dried mixed fruit
1 medium onion, thinly sliced
1 bay leaf
¾ tsp. salt
½ tsp. pepper
½ tsp. dried rosemary, crushed
1½ lb. lean boneless pork, cut into 1-inch pieces
½ cup all-purpose flour
2 Tbsp. vegetable oil
1 cup apple cider

1. Place first 7 ingredients in a 5-qt. slow cooker.

2. Dredge pork in flour; brown in hot oil in a skillet over medium-high heat. Remove pork, reserving drippings in skillet. Place pork in slow cooker. Stir apple cider into reserved drippings; pour over pork.
3. Cook, covered, on LOW 6 to 8 hours. Remove and discard bay leaf.

Beef Brisket With Fall Vegetables

MAKES 8 SERVINGS
PREP: 18 MIN., COOK: 12 HRS.
This ingredient list looks long, but you probably have most of the items on hand. The result is worth the effort. Beau Monde is a ground seasoning blend. To make 2 Tbsp. for this recipe, combine 1 Tbsp. ground celery seed, 1½ tsp. onion powder, and 1½ tsp. salt.

2 (2-lb.) beef briskets, trimmed
2 tsp. salt
1 tsp. pepper
1 Tbsp. vegetable oil
4 carrots, peeled and cut into 2-inch pieces
3 parsnips, peeled and sliced
2 celery ribs, sliced
1 large onion, sliced
1 fennel bulb, quartered
12 fresh thyme sprigs
1 (1-oz.) envelope dry onion soup mix
1 (14-oz.) can fat-free beef broth
¾ cup dry red wine
½ cup ketchup
2 Tbsp. Beau Monde seasoning
8 garlic cloves
¾ cup chopped fresh parsley

1. Sprinkle beef with salt and pepper.
2. Heat oil over medium-high heat in a large nonstick skillet. Cook beef, in batches, 4 minutes on each side or until browned. Transfer to a 6-qt. slow cooker. Add carrots and next 5 ingredients.
3. Whisk together dry onion soup mix and next 6 ingredients. Pour mixture evenly over beef.
4. Cover and cook on LOW 12 hours or until tender. Transfer beef and vegetables to a serving platter. Pour remaining mixture through a wire-mesh strainer, reserving juices; discard solids. Serve beef and vegetables with juices. ◆

Ideas for Main Dishes

Answer "What's for dinner?" with one of these recipes.

Make the most of money-saving deals at your grocery store's weekly sales. Scan the ads, plan your meals, and purchase the main ingredients for these entrées when they are at a good price. Buy more than you need; cook enough for supper, and freeze extra for another week. A few of these recipes are make-ahead to allow time for marinating less tender, inexpensive cuts of meat.

Shrimp and Grits
MAKES 4 SERVINGS
PREP: 15 MIN., COOK: 10 MIN.

2 lb. frozen, peeled, deveined large shrimp
2 tsp. Cajun seasoning
1 tsp. dried Italian seasoning
1 tsp. paprika
¼ cup butter or margarine
2 garlic cloves, pressed
1 cup chicken broth, divided
2 tsp. Worcestershire sauce
1 tsp. hot sauce
2 tsp. all-purpose flour
Hot cooked grits

1. Thaw shrimp according to package directions. Rinse and drain well.
2. Combine Cajun seasoning, Italian seasoning, and paprika in a large bowl; add shrimp, and toss to coat.
3. Melt butter in a large skillet over medium heat; add garlic, and sauté 1 minute. Add shrimp, ¾ cup broth, Worcestershire sauce, and hot sauce; cook 5 minutes or just until shrimp turn pink. Remove shrimp with a slotted spoon, reserving broth mixture in skillet.
4. Whisk together flour and remaining ¼ cup chicken broth until blended; whisk flour mixture into broth mixture in skillet, and cook, whisking constantly, 2 to 3 minutes or until thickened. Add shrimp, and cook 1 minute. Serve immediately over hot grits.

Cilantro-Garlic Sirloin With Zesty Corn Salsa
MAKES 8 SERVINGS
PREP: 15 MIN., STAND: 40 MIN., GRILL: 24 MIN.

1 cup (1 bunch) fresh cilantro, packed
2 Tbsp. olive oil
2 garlic cloves
1 Tbsp. grated lime rind
3 Tbsp. fresh lime juice
½ tsp. salt
½ tsp. ground cumin
¼ to ½ tsp. ground red pepper
2 lb. top sirloin steak (1¼ inches thick)
Zesty Corn Salsa

1. Process first 8 ingredients in a food processor or blender until blended. Rub cilantro mixture over sirloin steak. Let stand at room temperature 30 minutes, or cover and chill up to 8 hours.

2. Grill, covered with grill lid, over medium-high heat (350° to 400°) 10 to 12 minutes on each side or to desired degree of doneness. Let steak stand 10 minutes.

3. Cut steak diagonally across the grain into thin strips. Serve with Zesty Corn Salsa.

Zesty Corn Salsa:
MAKES 2 CUPS
PREP: 10 MIN.

---

3 cups frozen shoepeg white corn, thawed
½ medium red bell pepper, diced
1 small jalapeño pepper, minced
1 Tbsp. olive oil
½ tsp. grated lime rind
¼ cup fresh lime juice
¼ tsp. salt
¼ tsp. ground cumin

---

1. Stir together all ingredients.

Grilled Pork Cosmopolitan Salad

MAKES 6 TO 8 SERVINGS
PREP: 15 MIN., COOK: 5 MIN., CHILL: 15 MIN., GRILL: 20 MIN., STAND: 10 MIN.
This tasty recipe is based on the ever-cool, colorful Cosmopolitan cocktail.

¼ cup jellied cranberry sauce
¼ cup orange marmalade
⅓ cup orange juice
¼ cup fresh lime juice (about 3 limes)
¼ cup peanut oil
2¼ tsp. salt, divided
2 Tbsp. vodka
1 Tbsp. minced or grated fresh ginger
2 (1-lb.) packages pork tenderloins
2 tsp. lemon pepper
½ tsp. ground red pepper
2 (10-oz.) packages European blend salad greens
½ cup dried cranberries
1 (11-oz.) can mandarin oranges, drained

---

1. Whisk together cranberry sauce and marmalade in a small saucepan over low heat until melted. Remove from heat. Whisk in orange juice, lime juice, and oil. Reserve ½ cup of cranberry mixture, and add ¼ tsp. salt; set aside. Pour remaining cranberry mixture into a shallow dish or zip-top plastic bag; add vodka, ginger, and pork, turning to coat all sides. Cover or seal, and chill 15 minutes, turning occasionally. Remove pork from marinade, discarding marinade.

2. Stir together lemon pepper, ground red pepper, and remaining 2 tsp. salt; sprinkle evenly over pork.

3. Grill, covered with grill lid, over medium-high heat (350° to 400°) 10 minutes on each side or until a meat thermometer inserted in thickest portion registers 155°. Remove from grill, and cover with aluminum foil. Let stand 10 minutes. Cut pork diagonally into ¼-inch-thick slices.

4. Toss together salad greens, cranberries, oranges, and reserved ½ cup cranberry mixture; serve with pork.

Broiled Salmon With Dijon-Caper Cream Sauce

MAKES 6 SERVINGS
PREP: 10 MIN., BROIL: 7 MIN.
See page 8 for Fettuccine With Squash and Zucchini.

---

6 (6-oz.) salmon fillets
½ tsp. salt
1 tsp. pepper, divided
6 Tbsp. Dijon mustard, divided
1 (8-oz.) container sour cream
1 (3-oz.) jar capers, well drained
Garnish: fresh parsley sprigs

---

1. Sprinkle salmon with salt and ½ tsp. pepper; brush evenly with 2 Tbsp. mustard. Place on a lightly greased rack in a broiler pan.

2. Broil 5½ inches from heat 7 minutes or until fish flakes easily with a fork.

3. Combine sour cream, capers, remaining ½ tsp. pepper, and remaining 4 Tbsp. mustard. Serve over salmon. Garnish, if desired. ▶

Broiled Salmon With Dijon-Caper Cream Sauce over Fettuccine With Squash and Zucchini

Steak Stir-fry

¼ tsp. salt in a large shallow dish; add steaks, turning to coat. Cover and chill 30 minutes, turning once.

2. Remove steaks from marinade, discarding marinade. Sprinkle steaks evenly with remaining ¼ tsp. salt and ½ tsp. black pepper.

3. Grill steaks, covered with grill lid, over medium-high heat (350° to 400°) 4 to 5 minutes on each side or to desired degree of doneness. Serve grilled steaks with Spicy Herb Sauce.

Spicy Herb Sauce:

MAKES ABOUT 1 CUP
PREP: 15 MIN.

⅔ cup loosely packed fresh
   cilantro leaves
3 garlic cloves, minced
1 small jalapeño pepper, seeded
   and coarsely chopped
⅓ cup vegetable oil
3 Tbsp. soy sauce
1½ Tbsp. fresh lime juice
¼ tsp. sesame oil

1. Process cilantro leaves and remaining ingredients in a blender or food processor 20 seconds or until smooth, stopping to scrape down sides.

Spicy Brown Mustard Pork Chops

MAKES 6 SERVINGS
PREP: 10 MIN., COOK: 6 MIN.

½ tsp. salt
½ tsp. garlic powder
¼ tsp. pepper
½ cup spicy brown mustard*
6 (½-inch-thick) boneless pork
   chops
1 cup all-purpose flour
¼ cup vegetable or canola oil

1. Combine first 3 ingredients. Spread mustard evenly on both sides of pork chops; sprinkle evenly with salt mixture.
2. Place flour in a shallow dish; dredge pork chops in flour.
3. Cook pork chops in hot oil in a large skillet over medium-high heat 2 to 3 minutes on each side or until golden brown. Drain on paper towels, and serve immediately.

*Dijon mustard or coarse-grained mustard may be substituted.

Steak Stir-fry

MAKES 4 SERVINGS
PREP: 20 MIN., COOK: 12 MIN.

¾ cup beef broth
¼ cup lite soy sauce
1 Tbsp. cornstarch
1¼ lb. boneless top sirloin steak
¼ cup vegetable oil
1 garlic clove, minced
1 tsp. ground ginger
½ tsp. salt
½ tsp. pepper
1 large green bell pepper, cut into
   strips
1 large red bell pepper, cut into
   strips
1 large onion, thinly sliced
1 (8-oz.) can sliced water
   chestnuts, drained
4 green onions, cut into 1-inch
   pieces
Hot cooked rice

1. Stir together first 3 ingredients in a small bowl; set aside.
2. Trim excess fat from steak. Slice diagonally across grain into thin strips.
3. Pour oil around top of preheated wok or skillet, coating sides; heat at medium-high 2 minutes. Add garlic and next 3 ingredients; stir-fry 1 minute. Add steak to wok; stir-fry 2 minutes or until no longer pink. Remove steak from wok with a slotted spoon, and drain on paper towels.
4. Add pepper strips and onion to wok; stir-fry 5 minutes or until crisp-tender. Add steak, water chestnuts, green onions, and reserved beef broth mixture; stir-fry 2 minutes or until mixture is thickened. Serve over rice.

Asian Grilled Steaks With Spicy Herb Sauce

MAKES 6 SERVINGS
PREP: 20 MIN., CHILL: 30 MIN.,
GRILL: 10 MIN.

⅔ cup vegetable oil
3 garlic cloves, minced
3 Tbsp. sugar
3 Tbsp. cooking sherry
1 Tbsp. sesame oil
1 tsp. dried crushed red pepper
½ tsp. salt, divided
6 (1-inch-thick) beef strip steaks
½ tsp. ground black pepper
Spicy Herb Sauce

1. Whisk together first 6 ingredients and

Crispy Catfish With Pecan Tartar Sauce

MAKES 4 SERVINGS
PREP: 20 MIN., CHILL: 8 HRS.,
FRY: 6 MIN. PER BATCH

make ahead

---

4 (6-oz.) catfish fillets
Milk
2 tsp. hot sauce
2 tsp. salt, divided
1 large egg
¾ cup all-purpose flour
1 tsp. ground red pepper
1 tsp. ground black pepper
1 cup pecans, finely chopped
Vegetable oil
Pecan Tartar Sauce

---

1. Combine catfish and milk to cover in a shallow dish or large zip-top plastic bag; add hot sauce. Cover or seal and chill 8 hours, turning occasionally.
2. Remove catfish from milk mixture, reserving mixture; sprinkle catfish evenly with ½ tsp. salt, and set aside.
3. Whisk egg into milk mixture until blended.
4. Combine flour, ground peppers, and remaining 1½ tsp. salt. Dredge catfish in flour mixture, shaking off excess; dip in egg mixture, and coat with chopped pecans.
5. Pour oil to a depth of 2 inches into a Dutch oven; heat to 360°. Fry catfish 3 minutes on each side or until fish flakes with a fork. Drain on paper towels. Place on a serving platter, and serve with Pecan Tartar Sauce.

Pecan Tartar Sauce:

MAKES 1 CUP
PREP: 15 MIN., CHILL: 1 HR.
Use it for dipping, or spread it on a sandwich.

½ cup light or regular sour cream
½ cup light or regular mayonnaise
2 Tbsp. chopped toasted pecans
2 Tbsp. chopped fresh parsley
¼ tsp. grated lemon rind
1 Tbsp. fresh lemon juice
1 tsp. paprika
2 tsp. capers, drained and chopped
(optional)

---

1. Stir together first 7 ingredients and, if desired, capers. Cover and chill at least 1 hour.

Turkey Cheeseburgers

MAKES 8 SERVINGS
PREP: 20 MIN., CHILL: 30 MIN.,
GRILL: 12 MIN.

make ahead

These patties may be shaped ahead, wrapped in plastic wrap, and stored in zip-top plastic freezer bags in the freezer up to three months. Dark turkey meat mixed with turkey breast make these burgers tender and juicy.

---

1 lb. ground turkey breast
1 lb. ground turkey (dark meat)
1 large egg, lightly beaten
10 saltine crackers, finely crushed
3 to 4 green onions, sliced (about ½ cup)
2 tsp. salt
1 tsp. fresh or dried rosemary
¾ tsp. pepper
½ tsp. garlic powder
8 mozzarella cheese slices
8 onion buns, split
Tomato slices
Lemon Mayonnaise
Lettuce leaves

---

1. Combine first 9 ingredients until blended. Shape mixture into 8 patties. Cover and chill 30 minutes or until firm.
2. Grill turkey patties, covered with grill lid, over medium-high heat (350° to 400°) 5 to 6 minutes on each side or until done. Top each patty with 1 cheese slice during last minute of grilling.
3. Spread Lemon Mayonnaise evenly on cut sides of buns. Top bun bottoms, mayonnaise sides up, with lettuce, turkey patties, and tomato slices. Cover with bun tops, mayonnaise sides down.

Lemon Mayonnaise:

MAKES ABOUT 1 CUP
PREP: 5 MIN.

---

1 cup light or regular mayonnaise
½ tsp. grated lemon rind
1 Tbsp. fresh lemon juice
¼ tsp. pepper

---

1. Stir together all ingredients. Cover and chill until ready to serve. ◆

Turkey Cheeseburgers With Lemon Mayonnaise

Mini Mexican Meat Loaves

MAKES 6 SERVINGS
PREP: 20 MIN., BAKE: 40 MIN.

Individually shaped loaves are real crowd-pleasers, especially when offered with a choice of toppings.

1½ lb. ground beef
¾ cup mild picante sauce
1 (4-oz.) can chopped green chiles, drained
½ cup finely crushed corn chips
1 medium onion, chopped
1 large egg, lightly beaten
1½ tsp. ground cumin
1 tsp. salt
Picante sauce
1 cup (4 oz.) shredded Mexican four-cheese blend
Tortilla chips or corn chips
Garnishes: sour cream, chopped fresh cilantro

1. Combine first 8 ingredients, and shape into 6 loaves. Place on a lightly greased rack in a broiling pan.
2. Bake at 375° for 40 minutes or until done. Spoon desired amount of picante sauce over loaves, and sprinkle with cheese. Serve with tortilla chips or corn chips. Garnish, if desired.   ◆

Savory Pot Roast

MAKES 6 TO 8 SERVINGS
PREP: 20 MIN.; COOK: 7 HRS., 5 MIN.

make ahead

1 (3-lb.) beef sirloin tip roast, cut in half
2 Tbsp. vegetable oil
1 medium onion, chopped
2 garlic cloves, minced
1 cup brewed coffee
¾ cup water, divided
1 beef bouillon cube
1 tsp. salt
2 tsp. dried basil
½ tsp. coarsely ground pepper
All-purpose flour

1. Brown all sides of roast in hot oil in a large skillet over medium-high heat 5 minutes on each side. Place roast in a 4½-qt. slow cooker.
2. Add onion and garlic to skillet, and sauté 2 minutes or until tender. Stir in 1 cup coffee, ½ cup water, bouillon cube, and next 3 ingredients until blended. Transfer to slow cooker.
3. Cover and cook on LOW 6 to 7 hours or until tender. Transfer roast to a serving platter; measure drippings, and return to slow cooker. For every cup of drippings, add 1 Tbsp. flour to the remaining ¼ cup water. Whisk flour and water until blended. Whisk flour mixture into drippings. Cook, uncovered, on HIGH 5 minutes or until gravy thickens, whisking frequently. Serve gravy with roast.

---

menu

Savory Pot Roast over rice

Baby Spinach With Pine Nuts (page 11)

Cheese-Garlic Biscuits (page 27)

---

menu

Mini Mexican Meat Loaves with favorite toppings and chips

Texas Cake (page 87)

Smart Starts

When you read the dictionary's definition of convenience (something that makes life easier or more comfortable, especially a labor-saving device), you'll know what these recipes are all about. We're talking prepared sauces, dressings, fast-cooking foods, and prepackaged salad mixes and vegetables. We'll show you how to take advantage of all the tasty products available.

Vermicelli With Chunky
Vegetable Sauce

Use fresh ingredients to embellish a jar of sauce.

When it comes to marinara in a jar, here's a secret: Dress it up for homemade flavor. It's so simple. Just stir in fresh herbs, sautéed onions, garlic, mushrooms, and some browned ground beef or Italian sausage in a pot of simmering pasta sauce for a great meal. No one will know it's not from scratch. We won't tell.

Vermicelli With Chunky Vegetable Sauce

MAKES 6 SERVINGS
PREP: 20 MIN., COOK: 27 MIN.
If desired, stir in 1 lb. cooked ground beef or 2 cups chopped cooked chicken when you add the pasta sauce.

1 (16-oz.) package vermicelli
1 red bell pepper, diced
1 medium onion, diced
1 (8-oz.) package sliced fresh mushrooms
1 Tbsp. olive oil

2 small zucchini, diced

4 garlic cloves, minced

1 tsp. salt, divided

½ tsp. freshly ground pepper, divided

1 (26-oz.) jar tomato-and-basil pasta sauce

Freshly grated Parmesan cheese (optional)

1. Prepare pasta according to package directions; drain and keep warm.

2. Sauté bell pepper, onion, and mushrooms in hot oil in large nonstick skillet over medium-high heat 8 minutes; stir in zucchini, garlic, ¼ tsp. salt, and ¼ tsp. pepper. Cook, stirring occasionally, 4 minutes or until zucchini is tender.

3. Stir in pasta sauce, remaining ¾ tsp. salt, and remaining ¼ tsp. pepper; bring to a boil, stirring occasionally. Reduce heat, cover, and simmer 10 to 15 minutes. Serve over pasta. Sprinkle with cheese, if desired.

Chicken Parmesan

Meat Lover's Sauce

MAKES ABOUT 9 CUPS

PREP: 15 MIN., COOK: 35 MIN.

1 lb. ground chuck

1 lb. Italian sausage, casings removed

1 green bell pepper, chopped (about 1½ cups)

1 medium onion, diced (1¼ cups)

1 (8-oz.) package sliced fresh mushrooms

2 tsp. olive oil

2 (26-oz.) jars spaghetti sauce with roasted garlic

3 Tbsp. chopped fresh parsley

2 Tbsp. chopped fresh basil

Salt and pepper to taste

1. Cook ground chuck and sausage in a large Dutch oven, stirring until mixture crumbles and is no longer pink. Drain well on paper towels. Wipe Dutch oven clean.

2. Sauté bell pepper, onion, and mushrooms in hot oil in Dutch oven over medium-high heat 11 to 12 minutes or until pepper is tender and liquid is slightly reduced. Stir in beef mixture, spaghetti sauce, parsley, and basil. Bring to a boil, stirring occasionally; add salt and pepper to taste. Reduce heat, and simmer, uncovered, 15 minutes.

Giant Meatball Sandwich

MAKES 6 SERVINGS

PREP: 8 MIN., COOK: 30 MIN.,

BROIL: 2 MIN.

1 lb. ground chuck

½ lb. ground pork sausage

1 (14-oz.) jar spaghetti sauce with mushrooms and peppers (about 2 cups)

1 garlic clove, minced

1 (16-oz.) unsliced Italian bread loaf

1 (6-oz.) package provolone cheese slices

1. Combine ground chuck and sausage; shape into 1-inch balls. Cook meatballs in a large skillet over medium-high heat 8 to 10 minutes or until browned. Drain meatballs on paper towels. Discard drippings. Wipe skillet clean.

2. Combine meatballs, spaghetti sauce, and garlic in skillet; bring to a boil. Reduce heat, and simmer, uncovered, 12 to 15 minutes or until meatballs are done, stirring mixture occasionally.

3. Slice bread in half horizontally. Place bread, cut sides up, on a baking sheet. Broil 5½ inches from heat 1 to 2 minutes or until bread is lightly toasted.

4. Spoon meatball mixture over bottom half of toasted bread; arrange cheese on top of meatballs, overlapping as needed. Cover with top of bread. Cut sandwich into 6 pieces; serve immediately.

Chicken Parmesan

MAKES 4 SERVINGS

PREP: 15 MIN., COOK: 20 MIN.

4 skinned and boned chicken breasts

1 large egg, lightly beaten

⅓ cup Italian-seasoned breadcrumbs

2 Tbsp. butter or margarine

1 (26-oz.) jar spaghetti sauce with tomato and basil

¼ to ½ cup shredded mozzarella cheese

1 Tbsp. grated Parmesan cheese

1. Place chicken between 2 sheets of heavy-duty plastic wrap; flatten to a ¼-inch thickness using a meat mallet or rolling pin. Dip chicken in egg; dredge in breadcrumbs.

2. Melt butter in a skillet over medium-high heat; add chicken, and cook 2 minutes on each side or until browned.

3. Pour spaghetti sauce over chicken. Cover, reduce heat, and simmer 10 minutes. Sprinkle with cheeses. Cover and simmer 5 minutes or until cheese melts. ◆

Quick Bean Soup

Add a spicy kick to recipes with no fuss.

Prepared salsa or picante is what most of us pull out to serve with tortilla chips on a moment's notice, but this Southwestern staple also adds zesty flavor to weeknight dishes. Choose your favorite salsa with the spiciness level you prefer—mild, medium, or hot.

Quick Bean Soup

MAKES 10 CUPS
PREP: 15 MIN., COOK: 15 MIN.

---

1 large onion, chopped
1 small green bell pepper, chopped
2 tsp. vegetable oil
1 (15-oz.) can kidney beans, rinsed and drained
1 (15-oz.) can pinto beans, rinsed and drained
1 (15-oz.) can black beans, rinsed and drained
2 (14½-oz.) cans no-salt-added stewed tomatoes, undrained
1 (14½-oz.) can fat-free chicken broth
1 cup picante sauce
1 tsp. ground cumin

---

1. Sauté onion and bell pepper in hot oil in a large saucepan until tender. Add kidney beans and remaining ingredients; bring to a boil. Cover, reduce heat, and simmer 10 minutes.

Easy Skillet Tacos

MAKES 4 TO 6 SERVINGS
PREP: 10 MIN., COOK: 25 MIN.,
STAND: 5 MIN.

---

1 lb. ground beef
1 small onion, chopped
1 tsp. olive oil
1 Tbsp. chili powder
1½ tsp. ground cumin
1 tsp. salt
1 (15-oz.) can pinto beans, rinsed and drained
1 (8-oz.) can tomato sauce
¾ cup water
½ cup salsa
1½ cups (6 oz.) shredded Cheddar cheese
1 Tbsp. chopped fresh cilantro
Taco shells or flour tortillas, warmed
Toppings: shredded lettuce, diced tomatoes, salsa, sour cream

---

1. Cook ground beef in a large skillet over medium-high heat, stirring until beef crumbles and is no longer pink. Drain well. Remove ground beef; wipe skillet with a paper towel.
2. Sauté onion in hot oil in same skillet over medium-high heat. Add chili powder, cumin, salt, and ground beef. Cook, stirring occasionally, 5 to 7 minutes. Stir in beans, tomato sauce, ¾ cup water, and salsa. Mash pinto beans in skillet with fork, leaving some beans whole. Bring to a boil; reduce heat, and simmer, uncovered, 8 to 10 minutes or until liquid is reduced.
3. Top evenly with cheese and cilantro. Cover, turn off heat, and let stand 5 minutes or until cheese melts. Serve with taco shells or tortillas and desired toppings.

Steak Sandwiches

MAKES 6 SERVINGS
PREP: 15 MIN., COOK: 15 MIN.

Add lots of hot, crisp steak fries for a casual meal.

---

3 Tbsp. butter or margarine
3 large onions, thinly sliced
3 Tbsp. vegetable oil
12 wafer-thin breakfast steaks
6 hoagie rolls, split and toasted
1 (8-oz.) jar picante sauce

1. Melt butter in a large skillet over medium-high heat; add onions, and cook, stirring constantly, about 10 minutes or until tender and lightly browned. Remove onions from skillet, and set aside. Wipe drippings from skillet.

2. Pour oil into skillet; place over medium-high heat until hot. Fry steaks, turning occasionally, 2 to 3 minutes or to desired degree of doneness.

3. Place 2 steaks on each hoagie roll bottom; top with onions, picante sauce, and roll tops.

Spicy Chicken Pasta

MAKES 4 SERVINGS
PREP: 15 MIN., COOK: 10 MIN.

This recipe makes great use of leftover chicken or rotisserie chicken from the deli.

---

8 oz. penne pasta
3 celery ribs, chopped
2 garlic cloves, minced
1 medium onion, chopped
½ green bell pepper, chopped
½ yellow bell pepper, chopped
3 Tbsp. olive oil
1 lb. skinned and boned chicken breasts, cubed

1 (16-oz.) jar salsa
1 Tbsp. dried parsley flakes
½ tsp. salt
¼ tsp. hot sauce

---

1. Prepare pasta according to package directions. Drain and keep warm.

2. Sauté celery, garlic, onion, and bell peppers in hot oil in a large saucepan over medium-high heat 3 to 4 minutes or until crisp-tender. Add chicken, and cook, stirring often, 3 to 4 minutes or until done. Stir in salsa; bring to a boil. Reduce heat, and simmer, stirring often, 2 minutes or until thickened. Stir in parsley, salt, and hot sauce. Serve over warm pasta.

Chicken-and-Refried Bean Tacos

MAKES 4 SERVINGS
PREP: 10 MIN., COOK: 15 MIN.

To save time, let folks assemble their own tacos.

---

1 (16-oz.) can refried beans
¾ cup salsa, divided
1 (10.7-oz.) taco dinner kit
½ medium-size green bell pepper, chopped

1 tsp. vegetable oil
2 cups shredded cooked chicken
½ cup water
8 (6-inch) flour tortillas
1 small tomato, chopped
1 cup (4-oz.) shredded Cheddar cheese

---

1. Microwave refried beans, ¼ cup salsa, and 1½ tsp. taco seasoning mix from dinner kit in a microwave-safe bowl at HIGH 1½ minutes or until thoroughly heated, stirring once. Set aside.

2. Sauté bell pepper in hot oil in a heavy skillet over medium heat 5 minutes or until tender. Stir in chicken, remaining taco seasoning mix, remaining ½ cup salsa, and ½ cup water. Cook, stirring occasionally, 8 to 10 minutes or until thoroughly heated.

3. Heat taco shells and tortillas according to package directions.

4. Spread about 2 Tbsp. refried bean mixture over 1 side of each flour tortilla, leaving a ½-inch border. Place 1 taco shell in center of tortilla, and press sides of tortilla up and onto sides of taco shell. Fill taco shells evenly with chicken mixture, tomato, and cheese. Serve immediately. ◆

Chicken-and-Refried Bean Tacos

Get big flavor from small doses of this creamy spread.

Peanut-Noodle Salad

Peanut butter isn't just for sandwiches. Stir it into savory dishes to thicken sauces and add a nutty sweetness. It's delicious in Asian-style pasta and marries well with pork or chicken. Think beyond bread and jelly, and use peanut butter to enliven your meals.

Peanut-Noodle Salad

MAKES 6 TO 8 SERVINGS
PREP: 25 MIN.

make ahead

This recipe can be easily halved for a side dish. Serve chilled or at room temperature. You can find soba noodles on the ethnic foods aisle at the grocery store.

2 large cucumbers
¾ cup lite soy sauce
½ cup coconut milk
½ cup rice wine vinegar
½ cup chunky peanut butter
4 garlic cloves, minced
1 tsp. sesame oil
½ to 1 tsp. dried crushed red pepper
½ tsp. salt
1 (16-oz.) package soba noodles or angel hair pasta, cooked
1 (10-oz.) package shredded carrots
6 green onions, cut diagonally into 1½-inch pieces

1. Peel cucumbers; cut in half lengthwise, removing and discarding seeds. Cut cucumber halves into half-moon-shaped slices.
2. Whisk together soy sauce and next 7 ingredients in a large bowl; add sliced cucumbers, pasta, carrots, and onions, tossing to coat. Cover and chill 8 hours, if desired.

Thai Green Apple Pork Lettuce Wraps

make ahead

MAKES 6 SERVINGS
PREP: 20 MIN., COOK: 15 MIN.

½ cup chopped Granny Smith
   apples
1 Tbsp. lemon juice
3 garlic cloves, minced
1 jalapeño pepper, seeded and
   minced
¼ cup diced red onion
3 green onions, sliced
1 Tbsp. vegetable oil
1 lb. ground pork
¼ cup chunky peanut butter
2 Tbsp. fish sauce
1¼ Tbsp. sugar
¼ tsp. salt
Iceberg or Bibb lettuce leaves

1. Toss chopped apple with lemon juice. Set aside.
2. Sauté garlic, minced jalapeño, ¼ cup diced red onion, and sliced green onions in hot oil in a large skillet 2 to 3 minutes or until vegetables are tender. Add pork to skillet, and cook, stirring constantly, 4 to 5 minutes or until pork is no longer pink. Stir in chunky peanut butter, fish sauce, sugar, and salt; cook, stirring often, until mixture is thoroughly heated.
3. Drain apple mixture, and stir into pork mixture. Serve in lettuce leaves.

Thai Green Apple
Pork Lettuce Wraps

Peanut Sauce

MAKES 2 CUPS
PREP: 5 MIN., COOK: 6 MIN.

Stir this sauce into cooked pasta, baste chicken or pork when grilling, or use as a dipping sauce for egg rolls or fresh vegetables.

1 small sweet onion, chopped
1 tsp. minced fresh ginger
½ to ¾ tsp. ground red pepper
1 tsp. vegetable oil
½ cup creamy peanut butter
1 cup water
1 Tbsp. soy sauce
¼ tsp. salt

1. Sauté first 3 ingredients in hot oil in a saucepan 1 minute; stir in peanut butter. Gradually stir in remaining ingredients; bring to a boil. Cook, stirring constantly, 3 minutes or until thickened.

Peanut Butter Dressing

MAKES 1⅓ CUPS
PREP: 10 MIN.

This easy dressing lends Asian flair to an ordinary salad.

⅔ cup vegetable oil
⅓ cup fresh orange juice
2 Tbsp. honey
2 Tbsp. creamy peanut butter
1 tsp. crushed red pepper
½ tsp. minced fresh ginger
¼ tsp. salt
Mixed salad greens

1. Whisk together first 7 ingredients in a bowl until blended and smooth. Serve over mixed salad greens.   ◆

Combine just a few fresh ingredients to make Peanut Sauce for grilling or dipping.

Add pizzazz to meals with bottled dressings.

Purchased dressings deliver extra taste to main dishes and salads. Some of these recipes call for only ½ to ¾ cup of dressing, making them a great use for the end of a bottle. Others require an entire container, so there will be no waste.

Sesame Pork over yellow rice

Sesame Pork

make ahead

MAKES 4 SERVINGS
PREP: 15 MIN., CHILL: 8 HRS.,
STAND: 30 MIN., GRILL: 28 MIN.

½ cup soy sauce
½ cup Russian dressing
2 Tbsp. sesame seeds
3 Tbsp. lemon juice
½ tsp. ground ginger
½ tsp. garlic powder
½ (1½-lb.) package pork tenderloins, cut into 1-inch cubes
2 yellow squash
2 small onions
1 green bell pepper
1 (15-oz.) can pineapple chunks, drained
Yellow rice (optional)
Garnish: parsley sprigs

---

1. Combine soy sauce and next 5 ingredients. Remove and reserve ½ cup mixture; cover and chill.
2. Place pork in a shallow dish or zip-top plastic freezer bag; pour remaining sesame mixture over pork. Cover or seal, and chill 8 hours. Let stand at room temperature 30 minutes before grilling.
3. Cut squash into ½-inch slices, onions into quarters, and bell pepper into 1-inch pieces. Arrange vegetables in a grill basket.
4. Grill vegetables over medium-high heat (350° to 400°) 15 to 20 minutes, turning occasionally and basting with ¼ cup reserved sesame mixture. Remove vegetables from grill basket.
5. Remove pork from marinade, discarding marinade. Arrange pineapple and pork in grill basket.
6. Grill over medium-high heat 4 minutes on each side, basting with remaining ¼ cup reserved sesame mixture.
7. Toss together vegetables, pork, and pineapple. Serve mixture over yellow rice, if desired. Garnish, if desired.

Texas Caviar

make ahead

MAKES 6 CUPS
PREP: 20 MIN.

---

2 (15½-oz.) cans black-eyed peas with jalapeño peppers, rinsed and drained
1 (10-oz.) can diced tomato and green chiles
2 avocados, diced
1 small green bell pepper, diced
½ red onion, diced
¾ cup zesty Italian dressing
1 Tbsp. fresh lime juice
¼ tsp. salt
Corn chips

---

1. Stir together black-eyed peas and next 7 ingredients. Cover and chill, if desired. Serve with corn chips.

Texas Caviar

Zesty Chicken-Pasta Salad

MAKES 4 SERVINGS
PREP: 20 MIN., CHILL: 1 HR.

8 oz. elbow macaroni
1 (12-oz.) bottle peppercorn-Ranch
    dressing
2½ cups chopped cooked chicken
1 (9-oz.) package frozen sweet
    peas, thawed
1 (2¼-oz.) can sliced ripe black
    olives, drained
1 pint cherry tomatoes, halved
Salt to taste

1. Cook macaroni according to package directions; drain and rinse with cold water.
2. Stir together cooked macaroni and remaining ingredients; cover and chill at least 1 hour.

Ranch House Fettuccine

MAKES 6 SERVINGS
PREP: 15 MIN., COOK: 25 MIN.

8 oz. fettuccine
1 (16-oz.) package fresh broccoli
    florets
1 medium red bell pepper, diced
2 Tbsp. olive oil
1 garlic clove, minced
¾ cup cooked ham, cut into thin
    strips
1 (6-oz.) package grilled chicken
    breast strips
4 sun-dried tomato halves in oil,
    drained and chopped
2 tsp. minced fresh rosemary
1 (8-oz.) bottle Ranch dressing
¼ cup freshly grated Parmesan
    cheese

1. Cook pasta according to package directions. Drain and keep warm.
2. Sauté broccoli and bell pepper in hot oil in a large skillet over medium-high heat 7 minutes or until crisp-tender; add garlic, and sauté 2 minutes.
3. Stir in ham, chicken, and tomatoes; sprinkle with rosemary. Cook, stirring occasionally, until mixture is thoroughly heated.
4. Toss together warm pasta, broccoli mixture, and ½ cup Ranch dressing; add cheese, tossing well. Serve with remaining Ranch dressing. ◆

Vegetable Patch Chicken Salad

MAKES 4 SERVINGS
PREP: 15 MIN., CHILL: 30 MIN.

3 cups chopped cooked chicken
½ cup cucumber-Ranch
    dressing
½ cup frozen tiny sweet peas,
    thawed
¼ cup peeled, seeded, chopped
    cucumber
2 Tbsp. minced onion
2 Tbsp. minced red bell pepper
2 Tbsp. minced fresh parsley
1 Tbsp. fresh lemon juice

1. Stir together all ingredients in a large bowl. Cover and chill at least 30 minutes before serving.

PHOTOGRAPHS: TINA CORNETT, WILLIAM DICKEY, BETH DREILING / STYLING: BUFFY HARGETT, MINDI SHAPIRO LEVINE / FOOD STYLING: ANGELA SELLERS

Smoky meat and sauces lead to easy dinners.

Warm Barbecue Salad With Barbecue Dressing

Warm Barbecue Salad

MAKES 6 SERVINGS
PREP: 10 MIN., BAKE: 35 MIN.

3 cups shredded cooked chicken*
Barbecue Dressing, divided
1 cup frozen whole kernel corn,
    thawed
2 bacon slices, cooked and crumbled
6 cups torn green leaf lettuce (about
    1 head)
4 plum tomatoes, chopped
⅓ large red onion, sliced
⅔ cup shredded mozzarella cheese

1. Stir together chicken and 1 cup Barbecue Dressing in a lightly greased 9-inch square pan.
2. Bake, covered, at 350° for 35 minutes or until warm.
3. Toss together corn and next 4 ingredients. Top with warm chicken mixture, and sprinkle with cheese. Serve immediately with remaining dressing.
*3 cups shredded barbecued pork may be substituted.

Barbecue Dressing:

MAKES 3 CUPS
PREP: 10 MIN., COOK: 20 MIN.

1 (18-oz.) bottle barbecue sauce
⅓ cup firmly packed light brown sugar
½ cup honey
⅓ cup ketchup
1 Tbsp. butter or margarine
1 Tbsp. Worcestershire sauce
½ tsp. seasoned salt
1 tsp. lemon pepper

1. Stir together all ingredients in a saucepan; bring to a boil. Reduce heat; simmer, stirring occasionally, 10 minutes. Store in refrigerator up to 3 months, if desired.

Black Bean Soup

MAKES 8 CUPS
PREP: 10 MIN., COOK: 30 MIN.

1 small onion, chopped
2 Tbsp. olive oil
2 garlic cloves, chopped
3 cups chicken broth
3 (15-oz.) cans black beans, rinsed
    and drained
1 (10-oz.) can diced tomatoes and
    green chiles

Leftover barbecue or purchased 'cue from your favorite joint isn't just for buns anymore, and neither is the sauce. We've rounded up a variety of recipes to satisfy your cravings for the sweet, smoky stuff by serving it up in new ways.

1 lb. shredded barbecued beef
2 Tbsp. red wine vinegar
Toppings: sour cream, shredded
  Monterey Jack cheese, chopped
  fresh cilantro

1. Sauté onion in hot oil in a Dutch oven over medium heat 5 minutes or until tender; stir in garlic, and sauté 1 minute. Stir in broth, beans, and tomatoes and green chiles; reduce heat, and simmer, stirring often, 15 minutes.

2. Process 1 cup bean mixture in a food processor until smooth. Return bean puree to Dutch oven; add beef, and simmer 10 minutes. Stir in vinegar. Serve with desired toppings.

Barbecue-Battered Chicken Strips
MAKES 6 TO 8 SERVINGS OR
16 APPETIZER SERVINGS
PREP: 20 MIN., FRY: 7 MIN. PER BATCH

3 lb. skinned and boned chicken
  breasts
3 cups all-purpose flour
1½ tsp. seasoned salt
1½ tsp. pepper
¾ tsp. garlic powder
2 cups buttermilk
¾ cup honey-smoked barbecue
  sauce
2 large eggs
Vegetable oil
Honey-smoked barbecue sauce

1. Cut each chicken breast into 3- x 1-inch strips, and set aside.

2. Combine flour and next 3 ingredients in a large, shallow dish.

3. Whisk together buttermilk, ¾ cup barbecue sauce, and eggs in a bowl. Dredge chicken pieces in flour mixture; dip in buttermilk mixture, and dredge again in flour mixture. (If flour gets gummy, just press into chicken pieces.)

4. Pour oil to a depth of 1½ inches in a deep skillet or Dutch oven; heat to 360°. Fry chicken, in batches, 5 to 7 minutes or until golden. Drain on wire racks over paper towels. Serve with extra sauce.

Barbecue-Battered Pork Chops: Substitute 3 lb. boneless breakfast pork chops for chicken, and proceed as directed. Serve in biscuits.

Skillet Barbecue Pork Chops
MAKES 6 SERVINGS
PREP: 10 MIN., COOK: 15 MIN.

6 (1-inch-thick) boneless center-cut
  pork loin chops
1 tsp. salt
½ tsp. pepper
2 Tbsp. vegetable oil
½ small onion, chopped
½ small green bell pepper,
  chopped
⅔ cup hickory-style barbecue
  sauce
½ cup orange juice
2 Tbsp. dark brown sugar
1 Tbsp. cider vinegar

1. Sprinkle pork chops evenly with salt and pepper.

2. Cook pork chops in hot oil in a large skillet over medium-high heat 1 to 2 minutes on each side or until browned. Remove chops from skillet.

3. Add onion and bell pepper to skillet, and sauté 5 minutes or until tender. Add barbecue sauce and next 3 ingredients, stirring to loosen particles from bottom of skillet until blended. Return pork chops to skillet; bring sauce to a boil. Cover, reduce heat, and simmer 4 to 5 minutes or until pork is done.

Easy Slow-cooker Brunswick Stew

MAKES 14 CUPS
PREP: 20 MIN.; COOK: 6 HRS., 30 MIN.

1 large onion, chopped
1 celery rib, chopped
1 large green bell pepper, chopped
1 cup frozen sliced okra, thawed
4 cups frozen cubed hash browns,
  thawed
¾ lb. chopped barbecued pork
  with sauce
1 cup chopped cooked chicken
1 (14½-oz.) can diced tomatoes,
  undrained
1 (15-oz.) can tomato sauce
1 (15¼-oz.) can whole kernel corn
  with red and green peppers,
  drained
1 (15¼-oz.) can lima beans, drained
2 cups chicken broth
½ tsp. salt
½ tsp. pepper
¼ tsp. Worcestershire sauce

1. Combine all ingredients in a 5-qt. slow cooker. Cook, covered, on HIGH 6 hours and 30 minutes.

Note: For testing purposes only, we used Ore-Ida Southern Style Hash Browns. ▶

Easy Slow-cooker
Brunswick Stew

Quick 'n' Easy Chicken
Barbecue Pizza

Quick 'n' Easy Chicken Barbecue Pizza

MAKES 6 SERVINGS
PREP: 10 MIN., COOK: 10 MIN.,
BAKE: 24 MIN.

1 small onion, chopped
½ red bell pepper, chopped
½ tsp. salt
¼ tsp. pepper
1 tsp. olive oil
1 (13.8-oz.) can refrigerated pizza crust dough
½ cup hickory-smoked barbecue sauce
2 (6-oz.) packages grilled boneless, skinless chicken breast strips
2 cups (8 oz.) shredded Monterey Jack cheese with peppers

Garnish: finely chopped fresh parsley
Hickory-smoked barbecue sauce

1. Sauté first 4 ingredients in hot oil in a large skillet over medium-high heat 8 to 10 minutes or until vegetables are tender. Drain well.
2. Unroll pizza crust dough; press or pat into a lightly greased 13- x 9-inch baking pan.
3. Bake crust at 400° for 12 to 14 minutes. Spread ½ cup barbecue sauce evenly over top of pizza crust in pan. Arrange chicken strips evenly over barbecue sauce; top with onion mixture, and sprinkle evenly with cheese.
4. Bake at 400° for 8 to 10 minutes or until cheese melts. Garnish, if desired. Serve with extra sauce.

Barbecue Pasta

MAKES 4 SERVINGS
PREP: 10 MIN., COOK: 18 MIN.
This unconventional combination of barbecue and a hearty pasta may become a new family favorite.

12 oz. penne pasta
3 Tbsp. butter
1 small onion, chopped
1 lb. shredded barbecued pork
1 cup barbecue sauce

1. Prepare pasta according to package directions. Drain and keep warm.
2. Melt butter in a 3-qt. saucepan over medium heat; add onion, and sauté until tender. Stir in pork and barbecue sauce; cook 10 minutes or until thoroughly heated. Serve over warm pasta.

Barbecue Quesadillas

MAKES 4 MAIN-DISH OR 8 APPETIZER
SERVINGS
PREP: 10 MIN., COOK: 12 MIN.

½ lb. shredded barbecued pork
8 (6-inch) flour tortillas
1 cup shredded Mexican four-
    cheese blend or Monterey Jack
    cheese with peppers
Salsa
Guacamole

1. Divide pork evenly among tortillas;
sprinkle each with 2 Tbsp. cheese. Fold
tortillas in half.
2. Cook quesadillas in a large nonstick
skillet over medium heat 3 minutes on
each side or until tortillas are crisp
and cheese melts. Serve with salsa and
guacamole.

Raspberry-Barbecue Chicken

MAKES 4 SERVINGS
PREP: 5 MIN., GRILL: 14 MIN.

4 skinned and boned chicken
    breasts
1 tsp. Creole seasoning
Vegetable cooking spray
Raspberry-Barbecue Sauce

1. Sprinkle chicken evenly with Creole
seasoning.
2. Spray cold cooking grate of grill
with cooking spray. Place cooking grate
on grill; grill chicken, covered with
grill lid, over medium-high heat (350°
to 400°) 7 minutes on each side or until
done, brushing Raspberry-Barbecue
Sauce evenly on 1 side of chicken
during the last 2 minutes of grilling.

Serve grilled chicken with remaining
Raspberry-Barbecue Sauce.
Note: For testing purposes only, we
used Tony Chachere's Original Creole
Seasoning.
Raspberry-Barbecue Sauce:
MAKES 1 CUP
PREP: 5 MIN., COOK: 7 MIN.

1 (10-oz.) jar seedless raspberry
    preserves
⅓ cup barbecue sauce
2 Tbsp. raspberry vinegar
2 Tbsp. Dijon mustard
1½ tsp. hot sauce

1. Bring raspberry preserves and next
3 ingredients to a boil in a small saucepan. Reduce heat to medium, and cook
2 minutes or until slightly thickened.
Stir in hot sauce.

Barbecue Scalloped Potatoes

MAKES 6 SERVINGS
PREP: 10 MIN., BAKE: 45 MIN.

3 large baking potatoes
    (about 2½ lb.)
1 (10¾-oz.) can cream of
    mushroom soup
1 (5-oz.) can evaporated milk
¼ cup spicy barbecue sauce
½ tsp. salt
¼ tsp. onion salt
2 cups shredded sharp Cheddar
    cheese
⅛ tsp. paprika

1. Pierce potatoes several times with
tines of a fork. Place on a microwave-
safe plate; cover with damp paper towels. Microwave at HIGH 6 to 8 minutes
or just until tender. Let cool slightly;
peel and slice.
2. Stir together cream of mushroom
soup, evaporated milk, ¼ cup barbecue sauce, ½ tsp. salt, and ¼ tsp. onion
salt until blended. Layer half each of
potato slices, barbecue sauce mixture,
and shredded Cheddar cheese in a
lightly greased 2-qt. round baking dish.
Repeat layers, and sprinkle top evenly
with paprika.
3. Bake at 350° for 45 minutes or until golden. ◆

Barbecue Pasta

This pantry staple tastes terrific in many dishes.

Jambalaya

Take advantage of all the convenience rice products on the market today. Instant rice isn't what it used to be. Soft, tender grains now come in a pouch that can be ready in seconds from the microwave. You'll save prep and cooking times without losing any flavor. Try jambalaya, a salad, a casserole, and meatloaf that all utilize this versatile ingredient.

Jambalaya
MAKES 8 SERVINGS
PREP: 20 MIN., COOK: 40 MIN.

1 lb. smoked sausage, cut into
    ¼-inch-thick diagonal slices
1 small onion, chopped
3 celery ribs, chopped
1 green bell pepper, chopped
1 garlic clove, minced
1 (14-oz.) can fat-free beef broth
¼ cup water

1 cup uncooked long-grain rice

1½ cups chopped cooked ham or chicken

1 (14½-oz.) can diced tomatoes, drained

1. Cook sausage in a Dutch oven over medium-high heat, stirring constantly, 7 minutes or until sausage is browned. Stir in onion and next 3 ingredients; cook, stirring occasionally, 2 to 3 minutes or until tender.

2. Add beef broth, ¼ cup water, and rice; bring to a boil. Reduce heat to low. Cover and simmer 20 minutes. Add ham and tomatoes, and cook, uncovered, 5 to 10 more minutes, stirring occasionally.

Note: For testing purposes only, we used Conecuh Original Smoked Sausage.

Kitchen Express: Omit broth and ¼ cup water. Stir in 3 cups cooked rice with ham and tomatoes. Proceed with recipe as directed.

Beef-and-Lime Rice Salad

MAKES 4 SERVINGS

PREP: 15 MIN., COOK: 35 MIN.

Serve this salad right away, or chill and serve cold.

1 lb. lean ground beef

1 tsp. salt, divided

3 cups water

½ tsp. cumin

1½ cups uncooked long-grain rice

1 tsp. grated lime rind

1 Tbsp. fresh lime juice

Toppings: salsa, shredded Cheddar cheese, sour cream, chopped tomatoes, chopped green onions, avocado slices

1. Cook beef and ½ tsp. salt in a 3-qt. saucepan over medium-high heat, stirring until it crumbles and is no longer pink. Drain and pat dry with paper towels. Wipe pan clean.

2. Add 3 cups water, ½ tsp. cumin, and remaining ½ tsp. salt to saucepan. Bring to a boil, and add rice; cover, reduce heat, and cook 20 to 25 minutes or until water is absorbed and rice is tender. Stir in cooked beef, 1 tsp. lime rind, and 1 Tbsp. lime juice. Serve salad with desired toppings.

Crispy Chicken-and-Rice Casserole

MAKES 8 TO 10 SERVINGS

PREP: 15 MIN., BAKE: 30 MIN.

2 (8.8-oz.) pouches ready-to-serve long-grain rice

2 cups chopped cooked chicken

2 (10¾-oz.) cans cream of mushroom soup

1 (8-oz.) can sliced water chestnuts, drained

1 (4-oz.) can sliced mushrooms, drained

1 cup chopped celery

¾ cup mayonnaise

1 small onion, chopped

½ cup sliced almonds

1 Tbsp. lemon juice

1 tsp. salt

1 cup crushed cornflakes cereal

1. Heat rice according to package directions. Combine rice and next 10 ingredients in a bowl. Spoon into a lightly greased 13- x 9-inch baking dish. Top with cereal.

2. Bake at 350° for 30 minutes or until golden and bubbly.

Note: Freeze up to 1 month. Thaw in refrigerator overnight. Bake, covered with foil, at 350° for 45 minutes. Remove foil; bake 15 more minutes.

Sesame-Turkey Meat Loaf

MAKES 4 TO 5 SERVINGS

PREP: 15 MIN., COOK: 2 MIN.,

BAKE: 50 MIN., STAND: 10 MIN.

¼ cup diced carrot

¼ cup diced celery

2 Tbsp. diced green onions

2 garlic cloves, minced

1 tsp. minced fresh ginger

2 Tbsp. dark sesame oil

1 cup cooked long-grain rice

¼ cup chopped water chestnuts

2 Tbsp. all-purpose Szechuan hot-and-spicy sauce

1 Tbsp. soy sauce

1 lb. ground turkey

2 Tbsp. sesame seeds

Chinese hot mustard or sweet-and-sour sauce (optional)

1. Sauté first 5 ingredients in hot oil in a large skillet 2 minutes or until tender.

2. Add rice and next 4 ingredients, combining just until blended. Shape into a loaf, and place in a lightly greased 8- x 4-inch loaf pan; sprinkle evenly with sesame seeds.

3. Bake at 350° for 50 minutes or until done, and let stand 10 minutes. Serve meatloaf with Chinese hot mustard or sweet-and-sour sauce, if desired. ◆

Beef-and-Lime Rice Salad

Jump-start supper with prepackaged produce.

Pasta With
Beans and
Greens

Mama always says, "Eat your vegetables." These days, that is simpler to do with prepackaged vegetables, salad greens, and slaw mixes. You'll save lots of time in the kitchen when you don't have to do all that chopping. Just open the bag, give the contents a quick rinse to freshen, and spin them in the salad spinner before beginning the recipe. You're set to toss with a dressing, stir into a soup, or sauté in a snap.

Pasta With Beans and Greens

MAKES 6 SERVINGS
PREP: 20 MIN., COOK: 32 MIN.

Besides being a delicious main dish, this recipe boasts generous amounts of protein, fiber, complex carbohydrates, iron, and calcium.

8 oz. uncooked bow tie
    pasta
1 large onion, chopped
1 (6-oz.) package portobello
    mushroom caps, halved and
    sliced*
1 Tbsp. olive oil
1 (6-oz.) package fresh baby
    spinach, chopped
1 cup low-sodium chicken broth
2 garlic cloves, minced
½ tsp. salt
½ tsp. pepper
1 (15-oz.) can great Northern
    beans, rinsed and drained
¼ cup shredded Parmesan cheese

1. Cook pasta according to package directions; drain. Place pasta in a large bowl; set aside.
2. Sauté onion and mushrooms in hot oil in a large skillet over medium heat 5 minutes. Add spinach and next 4 ingredients; cook, stirring often, 15 minutes or until spinach is tender. Add beans, and cook 1 minute.
3. Add bean mixture to pasta; toss gently. Sprinkle with cheese.
*1 (8-oz.) package sliced fresh mushrooms may be substituted.

Broccoli Slaw

MAKES 8 CUPS
PREP: 10 MIN., CHILL: 3 HRS.

make ahead

¼ cup cider vinegar
2 Tbsp. light brown sugar
½ tsp. salt
½ cup vegetable oil
1 (16-oz.) package broccoli slaw
2 small Rome apples, chopped
½ cup raisins

1. Whisk together first 3 ingredients in a large bowl; gradually whisk in oil. Add remaining ingredients, tossing well to coat. Cover and chill at least 3 hours.

Grilled Chicken With Sweet Soy
Slaw and Dipping Sauce

3 Tbsp. brown sugar
¼ tsp. pepper

1. Cook carrots in boiling water to cover in a large saucepan 15 minutes or until carrots are tender; drain and set aside.
2. Cook bacon in a skillet until crisp; remove bacon, and drain on paper towels, reserving 1 Tbsp. drippings in skillet. Crumble bacon; set aside.
3. Sauté onion in reserved drippings over medium-high heat 3 minutes or until tender. Stir in brown sugar, pepper, and carrots. Cook, stirring often, 5 minutes or until carrots are glazed and thoroughly heated.
4. Transfer carrots to a serving dish, and sprinkle with crumbled bacon.

Fruit Salad With Honey-Pecan Dressing
MAKES 4 SERVINGS
PREP: 5 MIN.

2½ cups fresh orange sections
2½ cups fresh grapefruit sections
1 avocado, sliced
3⅓ cups sliced strawberries
1 (16-oz.) package mixed salad greens
Honey-Pecan Dressing

1. Arrange fresh orange and grapefruit sections, sliced avocado, and sliced strawberries over mixed greens; drizzle with Honey-Pecan Dressing.
Honey-Pecan Dressing:
MAKES 1¾ CUPS
PREP: 5 MIN.

2 Tbsp. sugar
1 Tbsp. chopped sweet onion
½ tsp. dry mustard
½ tsp. salt
¼ tsp. pepper
¼ cup honey
⅓ cup red wine vinegar
1 cup vegetable oil
½ cup chopped pecans, toasted

1. Pulse first 7 ingredients in a blender 2 to 3 times until blended. With blender running, pour oil through food chute in a slow, steady stream; process until smooth. Stir in pecans. ◆

Grilled Chicken With Sweet Soy Slaw and Dipping Sauce
MAKES 6 SERVINGS
PREP: 5 MIN., COOK: 10 MIN., STAND: 10 MIN., GRILL: 16 MIN.
The dipping sauce will keep in the refrigerator, covered, for several weeks. Warm sauce over medium-low heat on the stove before serving. Use as a marinade for steaks or shrimp, too.

2 cups soy sauce
2 Tbsp. canola oil
8 pieces crystallized ginger
2 garlic cloves, minced
3 cups sugar
6 skinned and boned chicken breasts
2 (12-oz.) packages broccoli slaw
¼ cup green onions, chopped
1 Tbsp. sesame seeds, toasted
Salt and pepper to taste

1. Combine first 4 ingredients in a small saucepan over medium heat. Stir in sugar. Cook, stirring occasionally, for 10 minutes or until sugar dissolves.

Remove from heat. (Mixture will thicken.) Reserve 1½ cups soy mixture, and set aside.
2. Brush both sides of chicken evenly with remaining soy mixture; cover and let stand 10 minutes.
3. Grill, covered with grill lid, over medium-high heat (350° to 400°) 6 to 8 minutes on each side or until done.
4. Toss together broccoli slaw, green onions, sesame seeds, and ½ cup reserved soy mixture; top with grilled chicken. Season with salt and pepper to taste. Serve with remaining 1 cup reserved soy mixture.
Grilled Salmon With Sweet Soy Slaw and Dipping Sauce:
Substitute 6 (4-oz.) salmon fillets for chicken, and grill 4 to 6 minutes on each side or until fish flakes with a fork.

Glazed Carrots With Bacon and Onion
MAKES 4 SERVINGS
PREP: 5 MIN., COOK: 30 MIN.

1 (1-lb.) package baby carrots
3 bacon slices
1 small onion, chopped

Chicken-and-Wild Rice Casserole

make ahead

MAKES 6 SERVINGS
PREP: 10 MIN., COOK: 5 MIN.,
BAKE: 30 MIN., STAND: 10 MIN.

2 (8.8-oz.) pouches ready-to-serve long-grain and wild rice mix
1 (8-oz.) package sliced fresh mushrooms
3 cups chopped cooked chicken
⅔ cup Italian dressing
1 (8-oz.) container sour cream

1. Prepare rice according to package directions for 2 pouches.
2. Sauté mushrooms in a large, lightly greased skillet over medium-high heat 5 minutes or until liquid evaporates.
3. Stir together rice, mushrooms, chicken, Italian dressing, and sour cream; spoon into a lightly greased 2-qt. baking dish. Cover and chill 8 hours, if desired. Let stand at room temperature 30 minutes before baking.
4. Bake at 325° for 30 minutes or until thoroughly heated. Let stand 10 minutes.◆

Vegetable Lo Mein

MAKES 4 SERVINGS
PREP: 10 MIN., COOK: 15 MIN.

1 (7-oz.) package vermicelli
1 (16-oz.) package stir-fry vegetables
4 green onions, chopped
¼ tsp. dried crushed red pepper
2 garlic cloves, pressed
1 Tbsp. vegetable oil
¼ cup soy sauce
1 Tbsp. water
1 Tbsp. dark sesame oil
¼ tsp. salt
2 tsp. toasted sesame seeds

1. Prepare vermicelli according to package directions. Drain and keep warm.
2. Stir-fry vegetable mix and next 3 ingredients in hot oil in a large nonstick skillet over medium-high heat 4 to 5 minutes. Stir in soy sauce and 1 Tbsp. water; add pasta, tossing to coat. Remove from heat, and toss with sesame oil, salt, and sesame seeds. Serve immediately.

menu
Vegetable Lo Mein

egg rolls

fortune cookies

menu
Chicken-and-Wild Rice Casserole

Fruit Salad With Honey-Pecan Dressing
(page 55)

PHOTOGRAPHS: JOHN O'HAGAN / STYLING: MINDI SHAPIRO LEVINE / FOOD STYLING: ANGELA SELLERS

Main-Dish Chicken

The express lane to smart cooking begins with this versatile ingredient that you probably always have on hand. Start with chopped, cooked chicken or boneless, skinless chicken breasts for great-tasting meals with minimal fuss.

PHOTOGRAPH: WILLIAM DICKEY / STYLING: CARI SOUTH

Start With Cooked Chicken

Chicken Pot Pie

Chicken Pot Pie

MAKES 6 TO 8 SERVINGS
PREP: 35 MIN., COOK: 20 MIN.,
BAKE: 25 MIN.

For a decorative touch, cut out chicken or turkey shapes with cookie cutters in piecrust before fitting over chicken mixture. The openings allow steam to escape and help the dish cool faster. Do not cut slits into crust if making decorative cuts.

---

3 to 4 bacon slices
3 green onions, sliced
2 large celery ribs, chopped
½ cup all-purpose flour
2 (14-oz.) cans low-sodium fat-free
   chicken broth
3 cups chopped cooked chicken
   or turkey
3 hard-cooked eggs, sliced
3 carrots, cooked and diced
1 (8.5-oz.) can sweet green peas,
   drained
1 tsp. salt
¼ tsp. pepper
⅛ tsp. dried thyme
½ (15-oz.) package refrigerated
   piecrusts

---

1. Cook bacon in a large skillet until crisp; remove bacon, and drain on paper towels, reserving 3 Tbsp. drippings in skillet. Crumble bacon.
2. Sauté sliced green onions and chopped celery in hot bacon drippings in skillet over medium heat 5 minutes or until tender. Gradually whisk in ½ cup flour until blended. Gradually add chicken broth, and cook, whisking constantly, 3 minutes or until thickened and bubbly. Stir in 3 cups chicken, crumbled bacon, sliced eggs, diced carrots, green peas, and next 3 ingredients.
3. Spoon chicken mixture into a 3-qt. baking dish, and top with refrigerated piecrust; cut slits or shapes in top of piecrust.
4. Bake at 450° for 25 minutes or until crust is golden and bubbly.

When a recipe calls for chopped cooked chicken, try these solutions. Purchase a rotisserie chicken from the deli, which will give you about 3 cups chicken. Or go to the freezer, and take out chopped or shredded chicken that you've made ahead for just this occasion. (To make your own, see the box at right.) All of these dishes are great for weeknights, especially when you need to prepare something in a hurry.

Greek Chicken Salad With
Lemon-Herb Dressing

Greek Chicken Salad With Lemon-Herb Dressing

MAKES 4 TO 6 SERVINGS
PREP: 15 MIN.

3 cups shredded romaine lettuce
2 cups chopped cooked chicken
1 cup garbanzo beans, drained
2 tomatoes, cut into wedges
¾ cup kalamata olives, pitted
Lemon-Herb Dressing
1 (4-oz.) package crumbled feta
    cheese
Toasted pita bread triangles

1. Combine first 5 ingredients in a large bowl. Toss with Lemon-Herb Dressing; top with cheese. Serve with pita bread.

Lemon-Herb Dressing:

MAKES ABOUT ¾ CUP
PREP: 5 MIN.

3 Tbsp. lemon juice
½ cup olive oil
1 Tbsp. chopped fresh mint
1 Tbsp. chopped fresh oregano
1 Tbsp. chopped fresh parsley
½ tsp. salt
½ tsp. pepper

1. Whisk together all ingredients. ▶

make and freeze chopped cooked chicken

Choose one of these methods to cook chicken ahead of time. Let cool slightly, and chop or shred; place in zip-top plastic freezer bags or airtight containers, and freeze. Do the same if you have extra chicken after preparing a meal.

Basic Baked Chicken Breasts

MAKES ABOUT 8 CUPS
PREP: 15 MIN.; BAKE: 1 HR., 30 MIN.;
COOL: 10 MIN.

The chicken breasts we purchased for testing were on the large size—6 breasts totaled about 4¾ lb. Decrease the cooking time and pan size for smaller pieces.

4 celery ribs with tops, cut into
    4-inch pieces
2 carrots, sliced
2 medium onions, sliced
6 bone-in chicken breasts (about
    4 lb.)
½ tsp. salt
¼ tsp. pepper

1. Arrange celery, carrots, and onions in a lightly greased 15- x 12-inch roasting pan. Top with chicken; sprinkle with salt and pepper.
2. Bake, covered, at 350° for 1 hour to 1 hour and 30 minutes or until chicken is done. Cool chicken 10 minutes; remove and discard skin and bones. Chop meat, and store in airtight containers in freezer up to 3 months.

Boiled Chicken Breasts

MAKES ABOUT 8 CUPS CHICKEN AND 8 CUPS BROTH
PREP: 20 MIN., COOK: 45 MIN., COOL: 10 MIN.

6 bone-in chicken breasts (about
    4 lb.)

2 qt. water
1 small onion, quartered
2 celery ribs with tops, quartered
2 carrots, quartered
1 garlic clove
1 bay leaf
2 tsp. salt
1 tsp. pepper

1. Bring all ingredients to a boil in a Dutch oven. Cover, reduce heat, and simmer 30 to 40 minutes or until done. Cool chicken 10 minutes; remove and discard skin and bones. Chop meat, and store in airtight containers in freezer up to 3 months. Strain broth, discarding solids, and reserve to use fresh. Or freeze broth in airtight containers, if desired.

main-dish chicken

Chicken Flautas

MAKES 4 SERVINGS
PREP: 10 MIN., COOK: 8 MIN.,
FRY: 7 MIN. PER BATCH

½ cup water
1 tsp. chicken bouillon granules
1 Tbsp. cornstarch
¾ tsp. salt
½ tsp. pepper
1 large onion, chopped
2 garlic cloves, pressed
1 Tbsp. vegetable oil
2 cups shredded cooked
   chicken
1 (4-oz.) can chopped green chiles,
   drained

¼ cup chopped fresh cilantro
16 (6-inch) corn tortillas
Vegetable oil
Toppings: salsa, sour cream
Garnish: cilantro sprigs

1. Stir together ½ cup water and next 4 ingredients.
2. Sauté onion and garlic in 1 Tbsp. hot oil in a large skillet over medium-high heat until tender. Stir in cornstarch mixture, chicken, chiles, and cilantro. Cook over medium heat, stirring constantly, until thickened and bubbly.
3. Soften corn tortillas according to package directions; spread 2 Tbsp. chicken mixture in center of each

tortilla. Roll tightly, and secure with wooden picks.
4. Pour oil to a depth of 1½ inches into a large heavy skillet, and heat to 375°. Fry flautas, in batches, 7 minutes or until browned. Drain on paper towels. Remove and discard wooden picks. Serve with desired toppings. Garnish, if desired.

Cheesy Chicken Casserole

MAKES 4 TO 6 SERVINGS
PREP: 15 MIN., BAKE: 30 MIN.,
STAND: 5 MIN.
Place crackers in a zip-top plastic freezer bag, seal all but a small corner to allow air to escape, and crush with a rolling pin.

4 cups shredded cooked chicken
1 (10¾-oz.) can chicken-and-
   mushroom soup
1 (8-oz.) container sour cream
¼ tsp. pepper
1 (8-oz.) block sharp Cheddar
   cheese, shredded and
   divided
25 round buttery crackers, coarsely
   crushed

1. Stir together chicken, soup, sour cream, pepper, and 1½ cups cheese; spoon mixture into a lightly greased 2-qt. baking dish.
2. Combine remaining ½ cup cheese and cracker crumbs; sprinkle evenly over top.
3. Bake casserole at 350° for 30 minutes or until bubbly. Let stand 5 minutes before serving.

Chicken-Sausage Gumbo

MAKES 4 TO 6 SERVINGS
PREP: 20 MIN., COOK: 25 MIN.

½ lb. smoked sausage, cut into
   ½-inch-thick slices
1 to 3 Tbsp. vegetable oil
5 Tbsp. all-purpose flour
1 cup coarsely chopped
   onion
1 cup chopped celery
2 large garlic cloves, pressed
1 medium-size green bell pepper,
   chopped
2 cups chicken broth

Chicken Flautas

1 (28-oz.) can diced
   tomatoes
1 to 2 tsp. Creole seasoning
4 cups chopped cooked
   chicken
Hot cooked rice

1. Cook sausage over high heat in a Dutch oven, stirring often, 5 minutes. Remove sausage with a slotted spoon. Drain on paper towels.

2. Add enough oil to drippings in Dutch oven to equal 3 Tbsp., and whisk in flour; cook over medium-high heat, whisking constantly, 5 minutes. Add onion, celery, garlic, and green pepper; cook, stirring often, 5 minutes. Stir in broth, diced tomatoes, and Creole seasoning. Bring to a boil; cover, reduce heat, and simmer 5 minutes. Add sausage and chicken; simmer, covered, 5 minutes. Serve over rice.

Note: For testing purposes only, we used Conecuh Original Smoked Sausage.

Chicken Burritos

MAKES 4 SERVINGS
PREP: 25 MIN., BAKE: 15 MIN.

3 cups chopped cooked
   chicken
1 (1¼-oz.) envelope taco
   seasoning mix
1 (16-oz.) can refried
   beans
6 (8-inch) flour tortillas
1 (8-oz.) package shredded
   sharp Cheddar cheese
3 plum tomatoes,
   diced
1 small onion,
   diced
Salsa verde or salsa

1. Place chicken and seasoning mix in a large zip-top plastic freezer bag; seal and shake to coat.

2. Spread refried beans evenly down center of flour tortillas. Top with chicken, shredded cheese, diced tomatoes, and diced onion; roll up. Wrap each burrito in foil.

3. Bake at 350° for 15 minutes. Serve with salsa verde.

Creamed Chicken in Biscuit Bowls

Creamed Chicken in Biscuit Bowls

MAKES 8 SERVINGS
PREP: 10 MIN., COOK: 20 MIN.
You can also serve this over toast points, split biscuits, cornbread, waffles, or puff pastry shells.

2 Tbsp. butter or margarine
½ cup finely chopped onion (about
   1 small onion)
½ cup finely chopped celery
½ cup sliced fresh mushrooms
1 (10¾-oz.) can condensed cream
   of chicken soup
½ cup milk
¼ tsp. dried tarragon
1 cup (4 oz.) shredded sharp
   Cheddar cheese
2½ cups chopped cooked
   chicken
½ (16-oz.) package frozen peas
   and carrots, thawed
1 (2-oz.) jar diced pimiento,
   drained
¼ tsp. salt
½ tsp. pepper
Biscuit Bowls
Garnish: parsley sprigs

1. Melt butter in a large skillet over medium-high heat; add onion, celery, and mushrooms, and sauté 2 to 3 minutes or until tender. Whisk in cream of chicken soup, ½ cup milk, and tarragon; cook over medium-low heat, stirring occasionally, 3 to 4 minutes. Add

cheese, stirring constantly, until cheese melts. Stir in cooked chicken and next 4 ingredients. Cook over low heat, stirring often, 10 minutes or until thoroughly heated. Spoon warm chicken mixture evenly into Biscuit Bowls. Garnish, if desired.

Chicken Pot Pie in Biscuit Bowls: Substitute 1 (10-oz.) thawed package frozen mixed vegetables for peas and carrots. Add ½ tsp. dried thyme and ½ tsp. poultry seasoning. Omit tarragon, sliced mushrooms, and pimiento. Proceed with recipe as directed.

Biscuit Bowls:
MAKES 8 SERVINGS
PREP: 15 MIN., BAKE: 14 MIN.

1 (16.3-oz.) can refrigerated jumbo
   flaky biscuits*
Vegetable cooking spray

1. Roll each biscuit into a 5-inch circle.

2. Invert 8 (6-oz.) custard cups or ramekins, several inches apart, on a lightly greased baking sheet. Coat outside of cups with cooking spray. Mold flattened biscuits around outside of custard cups.

3. Bake at 350° for 14 minutes. Cool slightly, and remove biscuit bowls from cups.

*Frozen biscuits may be substituted. Let thaw at room temperature for 30 minutes. Biscuits may be slightly sticky; lightly flour before rolling out. Bake at 350° for 16 to 18 minutes. ◆

Tasty Dishes and Casseroles

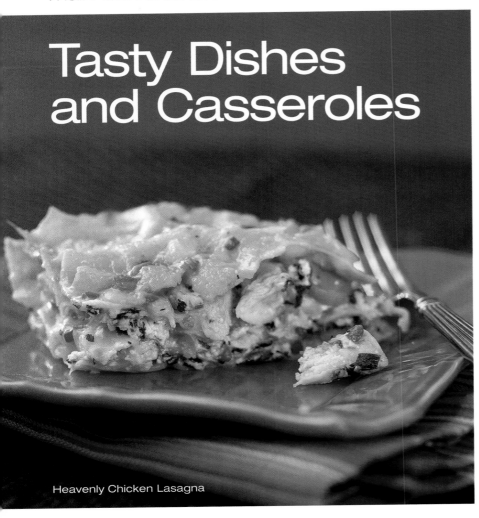

Heavenly Chicken Lasagna

We guarantee your family won't bolt from the table saying "not chicken again." Serve these tasty recipes, and we bet they will polish off every last bite.

Heavenly Chicken Lasagna

make ahead

MAKES 8 TO 10 SERVINGS
PREP: 30 MIN., COOK: 5 MIN.,
BAKE: 1 HR., STAND: 10 MIN.

1 Tbsp. butter
½ large onion, chopped
1 (10½-oz.) can reduced-fat cream of chicken soup
1 (10-oz.) container refrigerated light Alfredo sauce
1 (7-oz.) jar diced pimiento, undrained
1 (6-oz.) jar sliced mushrooms, drained
⅓ cup dry white wine
½ tsp. dried basil
1 (10-oz.) package frozen chopped spinach, thawed
1 (15-oz.) container ricotta cheese
½ cup grated Parmesan cheese
1 large egg, lightly beaten
9 no-cook lasagna noodles
3 cups chopped cooked chicken
3 cups (12 oz.) shredded sharp Cheddar cheese, divided

1. Melt butter in a skillet over medium-high heat. Add onion, and sauté 5 minutes or until tender. Remove from heat; stir in soup and next 5 ingredients. Reserve 1½ cups sauce; set aside.
2. Drain spinach well, pressing between layers of paper towels. Stir together spinach and next 3 ingredients.
3. Place 3 lasagna noodles in a lightly greased 13- x 9-inch baking dish. Layer with half each of sauce, spinach mixture, and chicken. Sprinkle with 1 cup Cheddar cheese. Repeat layers once. Top with remaining 3 noodles and reserved 1½ cups sauce. Cover and chill up to 1 day ahead, if desired. Let stand at room temperature 30 minutes before baking.
4. Bake, covered, at 350° for 50 to 55 minutes. Sprinkle with remaining 1 cup Cheddar cheese, and bake 5 more minutes or until cheese is melted. Let stand 10 minutes before serving.
Note: For testing purposes only, we used Buitoni Light Alfredo Sauce.

Creamy Poblano Chicken

MAKES 6 TO 8 SERVINGS
PREP: 10 MIN., COOK: 25 MIN.

3 Tbsp. butter or margarine
1 large sweet onion, chopped
2 poblano chile peppers, seeded and diced
3 garlic cloves, minced
8 skinned and boned chicken breasts, cut into bite-size pieces
1 tsp. salt
½ tsp. pepper
1 (10¾-oz.) can cream of chicken soup
½ cup chicken broth
1 (8-oz.) container sour cream
1 (8-oz.) package shredded sharp Cheddar cheese

1. Melt butter in a Dutch oven over medium-high heat. Add onion, poblanos, and garlic; sauté 5 minutes. Add chicken, salt, and pepper; cook, stirring often, 8 to 10 minutes or until chicken is done. Stir in soup, broth, and sour cream. Add cheese; cook 7 to 8 minutes.

Pesto-Chicken Cheesecakes

make ahead

MAKES 4 SERVINGS
PREP: 15 MIN., BAKE: 20 MIN.

2 (8-oz.) packages cream cheese, softened
2 large eggs
2 Tbsp. all-purpose flour
3 Tbsp. prepared basil pesto
1 cup chopped cooked chicken
Mixed salad greens
1 (8-oz.) container sour cream
Garnish: chopped fresh chives

1. Beat cream cheese at medium speed with an electric mixer until smooth. Add eggs, flour, and pesto, beating until blended. Stir in chicken. Pour into 4 (4-inch) ramekins. Cover and chill 8 hours, if desired. Let stand at room temperature 30 minutes before baking.
2. Bake at 325° for 20 minutes. Gently run a knife around edges of cheesecakes; invert ramekins, and unmold cheesecakes onto mixed salad greens. Spread sour cream evenly over tops of cheesecakes. Cheesecakes may be served hot or cold. Garnish, if desired.

Chicken Diane

MAKES 4 SERVINGS
PREP: 25 MIN., COOK: 10 MIN.

4 skinned and boned chicken breasts
½ tsp. salt
¼ tsp. pepper
1 Tbsp. butter
1 Tbsp. olive oil
4 green onions, chopped
¼ cup chicken broth
2 Tbsp. lemon juice
2 Tbsp. brandy or chicken broth
2 Tbsp. Dijon mustard
3 Tbsp. chopped fresh parsley
Hot cooked rice

1. Place chicken between 2 sheets of heavy-duty plastic wrap; flatten to ¼-inch thickness using a meat mallet or rolling pin. Sprinkle with salt and pepper.
2. Melt butter in oil in a skillet over medium-high heat; add chicken, and cook 2 minutes on each side or until done. Remove chicken, and keep warm. Reduce heat to medium. Add onions and next 4 ingredients to skillet; cook, whisking constantly, until bubbly. Stir in parsley. Pour over chicken; serve with rice.

Cheesy Mexican Chicken

MAKES 4 SERVINGS
PREP: 10 MIN., COOK: 12 MIN.,
STAND: 3 MIN.

1 tsp. ground black pepper
¼ tsp. ground red pepper
½ tsp. paprika
½ tsp. garlic powder
4 skinned and boned chicken breasts
1 Tbsp. butter
1 (4.5-oz.) can chopped green chiles
1 cup (4 oz.) shredded Monterey Jack cheese
Paprika (optional)

1. Combine first 4 ingredients; sprinkle evenly over chicken.
2. Melt 1 Tbsp. butter in a large skillet over medium-high heat. Add chicken, and cook 5 to 6 minutes on each side or until done. Remove from heat, and top evenly with green chiles and shredded Monterey Jack cheese. Cover and let stand 2 to 3 minutes or until cheese melts. Sprinkle with paprika, if desired. ▶

Pesto-Chicken Cheesecakes

Fruity Baked Chicken

Chicken Spaghetti

MAKES 6 TO 8 SERVINGS
PREP: 15 MIN., COOK: 20 MIN.

1 (12-oz.) package spaghetti
1 medium onion, chopped
1 small green bell pepper, chopped
Vegetable cooking spray
1 (14¼-oz.) can chicken broth
1 (14¼-oz.) can Italian-style stewed
    tomatoes
1 (6-oz.) can Italian-style tomato
    paste
1 (16-oz.) package pasteurized
    processed cheese product, cubed
3 cups chopped cooked chicken

1. Prepare spaghetti according to package directions. Drain and keep warm.
2. Sauté onion and bell pepper in a Dutch oven coated with cooking spray over medium-high heat 3 to 4 minutes. Stir in broth, tomatoes, and tomato paste. Bring to a boil; reduce heat, and simmer 10 minutes. Stir in cheese; cook 1 minute or until melted. Stir in pasta and chicken; cook 2 to 3 minutes or until thoroughly heated.

Chicken-and-Broccoli Casserole

make ahead

MAKES 4 SERVINGS
PREP: 15 MIN., COOK: 15 MIN.,
BAKE: 25 MIN.

½ cup butter, divided
4 skinned and boned chicken
    breasts, cut into 1-inch pieces
1 (16-oz.) package fresh broccoli
    florets
¼ cup all-purpose flour
2 cups milk
½ cup (2 oz.) shredded Swiss cheese
½ cup (2 oz.) finely shredded
    Parmesan cheese
1 tsp. lemon juice
¼ tsp. salt
2 Tbsp. finely shredded Parmesan
    cheese

1. Melt ¼ cup butter in a large skillet over medium heat; add chicken, and sauté until done. Remove chicken from skillet, and set aside.
2. Cook broccoli in a steamer basket over boiling water 2 minutes or until crisp-tender. Remove from heat; drain well, and set aside.

Fruity Baked Chicken

MAKES 6 SERVINGS
PREP: 20 MIN., COOK: 10 MIN.,
BAKE: 30 MIN.

2 (6-oz.) packages long-grain and
    wild rice mix
2 tsp. salt, divided
⅓ cup all-purpose flour
½ tsp. pepper
½ tsp. paprika
6 skinned and boned chicken breasts
¼ cup vegetable oil
1 large sweet onion, diced
1 (7-oz.) package chopped mixed
    dried fruit
2 cups chicken broth
½ cup frozen orange juice
    concentrate, thawed
1 Tbsp. grated fresh ginger
1 tsp. chili-garlic paste
2 tsp. cornstarch
¼ cup water

1. Prepare rice mix according to package directions, omitting seasoning packets; add 1 tsp. salt. Set aside.
2. Combine flour, pepper, paprika, and remaining 1 tsp. salt in a large bowl. Dredge chicken in flour mixture.
3. Cook chicken in hot oil in a skillet over medium heat about 2 minutes on each side. Remove from skillet; set aside. Add onion to skillet; sauté over medium-high heat, stirring often, 5 minutes. Stir in fruit and next 4 ingredients; bring to a boil.
4. Combine cornstarch and ¼ cup water. Stir into fruit mixture; cook 1 minute.
5. Spoon rice into a lightly greased 13- x 9-inch baking dish. Place chicken over rice. Spoon fruit mixture over chicken.
6. Bake, covered, at 350° for 30 minutes.
Note: For testing purposes only, we used SunMaid FruitBits for dried fruit.

3. Melt remaining ¼ cup butter in skillet over medium heat. Whisk in flour, and cook, whisking constantly, 1 minute. Gradually add milk, and cook, whisking constantly, until thickened and bubbly. Remove from heat, and stir in Swiss cheese, ½ cup Parmesan cheese, lemon juice, and salt.

4. Layer half of chicken, broccoli, and cheese sauce in a lightly greased 11- x 7-inch baking dish. Repeat layer once. Cover and chill casserole up to 8 hours, if desired. Remove from refrigerator, and let stand at room temperature 30 minutes before baking.

5. Bake, covered, at 350° for 20 minutes. Uncover and sprinkle with 2 Tbsp. Parmesan cheese; bake 5 more minutes.

Sweet-and-Spicy Chicken Wings

MAKES 4 TO 6 SERVINGS
PREP: 10 MIN., COOK: 10 MIN.,
FRY 24 MIN., STAND: 5 MIN.

To save prep time, purchase chicken drummettes or a bag of frozen wings that are already separated.

1 (15-oz.) can tomato sauce
2 Tbsp. butter
½ cup honey
¼ cup chipotle-flavored hot sauce
1 Tbsp. grated lime rind
3 Tbsp. fresh lime juice
¼ tsp. ground red pepper
4 to 5 lb. chicken wings
1 Tbsp. salt
1 tsp. pepper
1 cup all-purpose flour
Peanut or vegetable oil

1. Heat tomato sauce and butter in a small saucepan over medium heat, stirring until butter melts. Stir in next 5 ingredients; bring to a boil. Reduce heat; simmer, stirring often, 5 minutes. Set aside.

2. Cut off wingtips; discard. Cut wings in half at joint, if desired. Sprinkle wings evenly with salt and pepper; dredge lightly in flour, shaking off excess.

3. Pour oil to a depth of 1½ inches into a large, deep skillet or Dutch oven; heat oil to 375°. Fry wings, in 3 batches, 8 minutes per batch or until golden and crispy. Remove wings from oil using a slotted spoon; drain on layers of paper towels. (Allow oil to return to 375° before adding next batch of wings.)

4. Place wings in a large bowl. Drizzle with tomato sauce mixture, tossing to coat. Let stand 5 minutes before serving.

Chicken and Bow Tie Pasta

MAKES 4 SERVINGS
PREP: 10 MIN., COOK: 30 MIN.

1 qt. salted water
4 skinned and boned chicken
    breasts, cut into bite-size pieces
8 oz. uncooked bow tie pasta
1 cup chicken broth
1 celery rib, chopped (about ½ cup)
1 small onion, chopped (about
    ½ cup)
1 (10¾-oz.) can cream of
    mushroom soup
1 (8-oz.) package pasteurized
    prepared cheese product, cubed

1. Bring 1 qt. salted water to a gentle boil in a Dutch oven. Add chicken, and cook 12 minutes or until done. Remove chicken from water with a slotted spoon. Return water to a boil; add pasta, and cook 10 minutes or until tender. Drain and keep warm.

2. Heat ¼ cup broth over medium-high heat in a Dutch oven; add celery and onion, and cook 5 minutes or until tender. Stir in chicken, soup, cheese, and remaining ¾ cup chicken broth, stirring until cheese is melted. Toss with warm pasta; serve immediately. ◆

Sweet-and-Spicy Chicken Wings

Chicken Dijon

MAKES 6 SERVINGS
PREP: 10 MIN., COOK: 25 MIN.
You may also serve this family favorite with a long-grain and wild rice mix and fresh, steamed broccoli spears.

6 skinned and boned chicken
  breasts
1 tsp. salt
½ tsp. pepper
3 Tbsp. butter
1 (14½-oz.) can chicken broth
1 medium-size sweet onion, diced
2 Tbsp. all-purpose flour
3 Tbsp. Dijon mustard

1. Sprinkle chicken evenly with salt and pepper.
2. Melt butter in a large skillet over medium-high heat; add chicken, and cook 2 minutes on each side or until golden brown.
3. Whisk together chicken broth and next 3 ingredients; pour over chicken. Cover, reduce heat to low, and simmer 20 minutes. ◆

menu
Chicken-and-Mushroom
Marsala

angel hair pasta

dinner rolls

Chicken-and-Mushroom Marsala

MAKES 6 SERVINGS
PREP: 15 MIN., COOK: 30 MIN.

6 skinned and boned chicken
  breasts
½ cup all-purpose flour
½ tsp. salt
½ tsp. pepper
2 garlic cloves, minced
¼ cup olive oil
1 (8-oz.) package sliced
  mushrooms
2 cups Marsala
Hot cooked angel hair pasta
Garnish: fresh parsley sprigs

1. Place chicken between 2 sheets of heavy-duty plastic wrap, and flatten to ¼-inch thickness, using a meat mallet or rolling pin.
2. Combine flour, salt, and pepper. Dredge chicken in mixture.
3. Cook half of chicken and half of garlic in 2 Tbsp. hot oil in a large skillet over medium-high heat 3 to 4 minutes on each side until done. Remove chicken; keep warm. Repeat procedure with remaining chicken, garlic, and oil, reserving drippings in skillet.
4. Add sliced mushrooms to skillet, and

sauté 4 minutes. Stir in Marsala, stirring to loosen particles from bottom of skillet; cook, stirring occasionally, 8 minutes or until liquid is reduced by half.
5. Return chicken to skillet, and cook until thoroughly heated. Serve over pasta. Garnish, if desired.

menu
Chicken Dijon

roasted potatoes

sweet peas

Bayou Brownies
(page 105)

Top-Rated Favorites

As a special treat, here's a collection of highly rated favorites for your weeknight meals and entertaining. These are tried-and-true gems that you will love. When you serve them, everyone will ask for the recipes.

Indulge in some of our finest from years past.

Beef Lombardi

The next time you entertain, impress your guests with one of these top-rated recipes. Or brighten an ordinary weeknight by treating your family to a terrific dish. After you try them once, these favorites are bound to become recipe box staples.

Beef Lombardi

make ahead

MAKES 6 SERVINGS
PREP: 10 MIN., COOK: 41 MIN.,
BAKE: 40 MIN.

1 lb. lean ground beef
1 (14½-oz.) can chopped tomatoes
1 (10-oz.) can diced tomatoes and green chiles
2 tsp. sugar
2 tsp. salt
¼ tsp. pepper
1 (6-oz.) can tomato paste
1 bay leaf
1 (6-oz.) package medium egg noodles
6 green onions, chopped (about ½ cup)
1 cup sour cream
1 cup (4 oz.) shredded sharp Cheddar cheese
1 cup shredded Parmesan cheese
1 cup (4 oz.) shredded mozzarella cheese
Garnish: fresh parsley sprigs

1. Cook ground beef in a large skillet over medium heat 5 to 6 minutes, stirring until it crumbles and is no longer pink. Drain. Stir in chopped tomatoes and next 4 ingredients; cook 5 minutes. Stir in tomato paste, and add bay leaf; cook 30 minutes. Discard bay leaf.

2. Cook egg noodles according to package directions, and drain. Stir together cooked egg noodles, chopped green onions, and 1 cup sour cream until blended.

3. Place noodle mixture in bottom of a lightly greased 13- x 9-inch baking dish. Top with beef mixture; sprinkle evenly with cheeses.

4. Bake, covered, at 350° for 35 minutes. Uncover and bake 5 more minutes. Garnish, if desired.

Note: Freeze casserole up to 1 month, if desired. Thaw in refrigerator overnight. Bake as directed.

To lighten: Substitute low-fat or fat-free sour cream and 2% reduced-fat Cheddar cheese. Reduce amount of cheeses on top to ½ cup each.

Beef Salad With Cilantro

MAKES 4 SERVINGS
PREP: 20 MIN., GRILL: 12 MIN.,
STAND: 10 MIN.

1 lb. boneless top sirloin steak
¾ tsp. salt
½ small red onion, sliced (about
    ¼ cup)
3 green onions, chopped
¼ cup chopped fresh mint leaves
¼ cup fresh cilantro sprigs
1 jalapeño pepper, seeded
¼ cup fresh lime juice
2 Tbsp. fish sauce
1 Tbsp. olive oil
1 Tbsp. brown sugar
½ tsp. red pepper flakes
1 medium head Romaine lettuce,
    chopped
¼ cup chopped peanuts

1. Sprinkle steak evenly with salt.
2. Heat a large cast-iron grill skillet over medium-high heat until hot. Grill steak 4 to 6 minutes on each side or to desired degree of doneness. Remove; cover lightly with aluminum foil, and let stand 10 minutes before slicing.
3. Combine red onion and next 9 ingredients in a large bowl, tossing to coat.
4. Slice steak diagonally across the grain into thin strips. Stir steak into onion mixture. Serve over Romaine lettuce. Sprinkle with peanuts.

Orzo Salad With Sesame Dressing

MAKES 6 SERVINGS
PREP: 20 MIN., COOK: 11 MIN.

1 lb. orzo pasta, uncooked
2 carrots, grated (about ½ cup)
2 Tbsp. chopped fresh cilantro
2 Tbsp. sliced green onions
Sesame Dressing
1 Tbsp. toasted sesame seeds

1. Cook orzo in boiling salted water 9 to 11 minutes; drain. Rinse with cold water; drain. Combine orzo, carrots, cilantro, and green onions in a bowl. Drizzle with Sesame Dressing, tossing to coat. Cover and chill. Sprinkle with sesame seeds.

Sesame Dressing:
MAKES ¾ CUP
PREP: 10 MIN.

¼ cup vegetable oil
¼ cup rice vinegar
1 tsp. sesame oil
1 tsp. soy sauce
1 Tbsp. sugar
1 Tbsp. grated orange rind
2 tsp. minced fresh ginger
1½ tsp. salt
½ tsp. minced garlic
¼ tsp. pepper
¼ tsp. dried crushed red pepper

1. Whisk together all ingredients until blended. Store in an airtight container in the refrigerator up to 1 week.

Grilled Southwestern Chicken With Pineapple Salsa

MAKES 4 SERVINGS
PREP: 10 MIN., GRILL: 8 MIN.
Serve with yellow rice garnished with chopped fresh cilantro.

4 skinned and boned chicken
    breasts
2 Tbsp. olive oil
1 Tbsp. chili powder
2 tsp. garlic salt
2 tsp. paprika
Pineapple Salsa

1. Place chicken between 2 sheets of heavy-duty plastic wrap; flatten to a ½-inch thickness using a meat mallet or rolling pin. Rub evenly with olive oil, and sprinkle evenly with chili powder, garlic salt, and paprika.
2. Grill chicken, covered with grill lid, over medium-high heat (350° to 400°) 4 minutes on each side or until done. Serve with Pineapple Salsa.

Pineapple Salsa:
MAKES 2 CUPS
PREP: 10 MIN., COOK: 4 MIN.

¼ cup diced red bell pepper
3 Tbsp. light brown sugar
2 Tbsp. chopped fresh cilantro
2 Tbsp. orange juice
2 Tbsp. fresh lime juice
1 Tbsp. chopped chipotle pepper in
    adobo sauce
1 Tbsp. butter
1 (15-oz.) can sliced pineapple,
    drained

1. Stir together first 6 ingredients.
2. Melt butter in a skillet over medium-high heat; add pineapple slices, and cook 2 minutes on each side or until golden brown. Coarsely chop; combine with bell pepper mixture. Store in an airtight container in the refrigerator up to 1 week. ▶

Beef Salad With Cilantro

Slow-cooker Chunky Beef Chili

MAKES 7 CUPS

PREP: 25 MIN.; COOK: 4 HRS., 15 MIN.

make ahead

3 lb. boneless chuck roast, cut into
½-inch pieces
6 tsp. vegetable oil
1 onion, chopped
1 Tbsp. chili powder
1 (6-oz.) can tomato paste
1 (32-oz.) container beef
broth
2 (8-oz.) cans tomato sauce
2 tsp. minced garlic
1 tsp. salt
1 tsp. ground oregano
1 tsp. ground cumin
½ tsp. ground black pepper
¼ tsp. ground red pepper
Toppings: crackers, sour
cream, shredded cheese,
chopped onion

1. Brown chuck roast pieces, in 4 batches, using 1½ tsp. hot oil per batch, in a large Dutch oven over medium-high heat. Add chopped onion, and sauté 5 minutes or until onion is tender. Stir in 1 Tbsp. chili powder; cook, stirring constantly, 1 minute. Stir in tomato paste; cook 3 minutes. Stir in beef broth, stirring to loosen particles from bottom of Dutch oven; stir in tomato sauce, minced garlic, and next 5 ingredients.
2. Carefully transfer meat mixture into a 6-qt. slow cooker. Cover and cook on LOW 4 hours or until chuck roast is tender. Serve chili with desired toppings.
Stove-Top Chunky Beef Chili:
Prepare recipe as directed, leaving meat mixture in Dutch oven; bring to a boil. Reduce heat to low, and simmer, uncovered, stirring occasionally, 1 hour and 30 minutes or until beef is tender. Serve with desired toppings.

Apple-Bacon-Stuffed Chicken Breasts

MAKES 4 SERVINGS

PREP: 15 MIN., COOK: 25 MIN.

2 bacon slices, diced
½ cup peeled, chopped
Granny Smith apple
½ cup dried cranberries, divided
1 Tbsp. fine, dry breadcrumbs
½ tsp. poultry seasoning
½ tsp. ground cinnamon
4 skinned and boned chicken
breasts
½ tsp. salt, divided
¼ tsp. pepper
3 Tbsp. butter
1 cup apple juice
2 Tbsp. apple brandy*
2 tsp. cornstarch
1 Tbsp. water
¼ cup coarsely chopped toasted
pecans
2 Tbsp. chopped fresh parsley

1. Cook bacon in a large skillet over medium heat until crisp; remove bacon, and drain on paper towels, reserving 1 Tbsp. drippings in skillet.
2. Sauté chopped apple in reserved hot drippings over medium-high heat 4 minutes. Remove from heat; stir in bacon, ¼ cup cranberries, and next 3 ingredients.
3. Cut a 3½-inch-long horizontal slit through the thickest portion of each chicken breast, cutting to, but not through, other side and forming a pocket. Stuff apple mixture evenly into each pocket. Sprinkle chicken evenly with ¼ tsp. salt and pepper. Wipe skillet clean.
4. Melt butter in skillet over medium heat. Add chicken, and cook 8 to 10 minutes on each side or until done. Remove chicken, reserving drippings in skillet, and keep warm.
5. Stir in apple juice, apple brandy, remaining ¼ cup cranberries, and remaining ¼ tsp. salt. Stir together cornstarch and 1 Tbsp. water until smooth; stir into juice mixture, and cook, stirring constantly, 1 minute or until thickened. Spoon over chicken, and sprinkle with pecans and parsley.
*2 Tbsp. apple juice may be substituted for apple brandy.

Slow-cooker Chunky Beef Chili

Grilled Maple Chipotle Pork Chops on Smoked Gouda Grits

MAKES 6 SERVINGS
PREP: 10 MIN., GRILL: 20 MIN.

We adapted this recipe from one of the finalists in our 2002 Cook-Off recipe contest.

½ cup barbecue sauce
½ cup maple syrup
2 chipotle peppers in adobo sauce, seeded and minced
1 tsp. adobo sauce from can
6 (1¼-inch-thick) bone-in pork loin chops
1 tsp. salt
1 tsp. pepper
Smoked Gouda Grits
Garnish: flat-leaf parsley sprigs

1. Whisk together first 4 ingredients; divide between 2 containers. Set aside.
2. Sprinkle pork chops evenly with salt and pepper.
3. Grill, covered with grill lid, over medium-high heat (350° to 400°) 10 minutes on each side or until a meat thermometer inserted into thickest portion registers 155°. Baste with half of barbecue sauce mixture the last 5 minutes of cooking.
4. Spoon Smoked Gouda Grits evenly onto 6 serving plates; top each with a pork chop, and drizzle evenly with remaining half of barbecue sauce mixture. Garnish, if desired.

Smoked Gouda Grits:
MAKES 6 TO 8 SERVINGS
PREP: 10 MIN., COOK: 15 MIN.

Buy a 7-oz. wheel of smoked Gouda cheese to get the right amount.

6 cups low-sodium chicken broth or water
2 cups milk
1 tsp. salt
½ tsp. ground white pepper
2 cups uncooked quick-cooking grits
1⅔ cups shredded smoked Gouda cheese
3 Tbsp. unsalted butter

1. Bring first 4 ingredients to a boil in a medium saucepan; gradually whisk in grits. Cover, reduce heat, and simmer,

Grilled Maple Chipotle Pork Chops on Smoked Gouda Grits

stirring occasionally, 5 minutes or until thickened. Add cheese and butter, stirring until melted.

Ginger-Glazed Pork Chops

MAKES 6 SERVINGS
PREP: 10 MIN., BROIL: 5 MIN., BAKE: 10 MIN., STAND: 10 MIN.

It's best to use fresh ginger found in the produce section, but 1 tsp. ground ginger may be substituted.

6 (½-inch-thick) bone-in pork chops
½ tsp. salt
⅓ cup apricot preserves
3 garlic cloves, minced
1 Tbsp. water
1 Tbsp. soy sauce
1 Tbsp. grated fresh ginger

1. Place pork chops on a lightly greased rack in an aluminum foil-lined roasting pan. Sprinkle evenly with salt.
2. Combine preserves and next 4 ingredients. Spread evenly over pork.
3. Broil 6 inches from heat 5 minutes. Reduce oven temperature to 425°. Bake 8 to 10 minutes or until a meat thermometer inserted into thickest portion registers 155°. Remove from oven; cover and let stand 10 minutes or until thermometer registers 160°.

Ginger-Glazed Pork Tenderloin: Substitute 1 (2-lb.) pork tenderloin for pork chops. Prepare pork as directed. Do not broil. Bake at 425° for 25 minutes or until a meat thermometer inserted in thickest portion registers 155°. Remove from oven; cover and let stand 10 minutes or until thermometer registers 160°. Makes 6 servings. Prep: 10 min., Bake: 25 min., Stand: 10 min.

Orange-Spice Mashed Sweet Potatoes

MAKES 4 TO 6 SERVINGS
PREP: 15 MIN., COOK: 10 MIN.

1 (29-oz.) can cut sweet potatoes
¼ cup orange juice
¼ cup milk
1 tsp. grated orange rind
¼ tsp. ground cinnamon
⅛ tsp. ground nutmeg
⅛ tsp. ground ginger
Garnish: grated orange rind

1. Cook sweet potatoes and orange juice over medium-high heat in a medium saucepan 10 minutes or until thoroughly heated. Drain and return potatoes to pan. Add milk and next 4 ingredients. Beat at medium speed with an electric mixer until smooth. Garnish, if desired. ▶

Florentine Artichoke Dip

Florentine Artichoke Dip

MAKES 4 CUPS
PREP: 10 MIN., BAKE: 25 MIN.

1 (10-oz.) package frozen chopped
   spinach, thawed
2 (6-oz.) jars marinated artichoke
   hearts
3 garlic cloves, minced
½ cup light mayonnaise
1½ (8-oz.) packages cream
   cheese, softened
2 Tbsp. lemon juice
1 tsp. hot sauce
¼ cup fine, dry breadcrumbs
1 cup grated Parmesan cheese
Crackers or breadsticks

1. Drain spinach well; press between paper towels. Drain and chop artichoke hearts.
2. Combine spinach, artichoke hearts, garlic, and next 4 ingredients, stirring well. Spoon into a lightly greased 11- x 7-inch baking dish; sprinkle evenly with breadcrumbs and Parmesan cheese.
3. Bake at 375° for 25 minutes, and serve with crackers or breadsticks.

Smashed Pinto Beans

MAKES 8 SERVINGS
PREP: 15 MIN., COOK: 20 MIN.
Keep these fiber-rich beans on hand to assemble quick breakfast burritos or veggie tacos.

1 medium onion, chopped
1 tsp. olive oil
2 garlic cloves, minced
½ cup tomato sauce
2 (15-oz.) cans pinto beans, rinsed
   and drained
1 cup beef broth
1 Tbsp. hot sauce
¼ tsp. salt
¼ tsp. ground cumin
½ tsp. pepper
1 to 2 Tbsp. red wine vinegar

1. Sauté onion in hot oil in a Dutch oven over medium-high heat 5 minutes or until tender. Add garlic, and sauté 1 minute. Stir in tomato sauce and remaining ingredients. Bring to a boil; reduce heat, and simmer 8 minutes.
2. Mash bean mixture with a potato masher until thickened, leaving some beans whole.

Leslie's Favorite Chicken-and-Wild Rice Casserole

MAKES 6 TO 8 SERVINGS
PREP: 30 MIN., COOK 10 MIN.,
BAKE: 35 MIN.

make ahead

2 (6.2-oz.) packages fast-cooking
   long-grain and wild rice mix
¼ cup butter
2 medium onions, chopped
4 celery ribs, chopped
2 (8-oz.) cans sliced water
   chestnuts, drained
5 cups chopped cooked chicken
4 cups (16 oz.) shredded Cheddar
   cheese, divided
2 (10¾-oz.) cans cream of
   mushroom soup
2 (8-oz.) containers sour cream
1 cup milk
½ tsp. salt
½ tsp. pepper
½ cup soft breadcrumbs (optional)

1. Prepare rice according to package directions. Set aside.

2. Melt butter in a large skillet over medium heat; add onions, celery, and water chestnuts. Sauté 10 minutes or until tender.

3. Stir in rice, chicken, 3 cups cheese, and next 5 ingredients; spoon mixture into a lightly greased 15- x 10-inch baking dish or a 4-qt. baking dish. Top evenly with breadcrumbs, if desired.

4. Bake casserole at 350° for 30 minutes. Sprinkle with remaining 1 cup cheese, and bake 5 more minutes.

Note: Casserole may be frozen up to 1 month. Let stand at room temperature 1 hour. Bake, covered, at 350° for 30 minutes. Uncover and bake 55 more minutes. Sprinkle with 1 cup cheese, and bake 5 more minutes.

Pork Scaloppine
MAKES 4 SERVINGS
PREP: 25 MIN., COOK: 15 MIN.

1½ lb. pork tenderloin*
½ tsp. salt
⅛ tsp. pepper
2 large eggs
¼ cup milk
½ cup freshly grated Romano
  cheese
½ tsp. garlic powder
¾ cup Italian-seasoned
  breadcrumbs
¼ cup butter
¼ cup olive oil
1 (8-oz.) package sliced fresh
  mushrooms
½ cup Madeira or dry white wine
1 (14-oz.) can chicken broth
Salt and pepper to taste

1. Cut pork into ½-inch-thick slices. Place pork between 2 sheets of heavy-duty plastic wrap, and flatten to a ¼-inch thickness using a meat mallet or rolling pin. Sprinkle evenly with salt and pepper.

2. Whisk together eggs and milk. Combine cheese, garlic powder, and breadcrumbs. Dip pork in egg mixture, and dredge in breadcrumb mixture.

3. Melt butter with olive oil in a large skillet over medium-high heat. Cook pork, in batches, 1 minute on each side or until browned. Remove pork, and reserve 1 Tbsp. drippings in skillet.

4. Sauté mushrooms in hot drippings in skillet over medium-high heat 4 minutes. Add wine, stirring to loosen particles from bottom of skillet; cook 2 minutes. Stir in broth; bring to a boil. Reduce heat; simmer 5 minutes or until thickened. Season with salt and pepper to taste. Spoon over pork; serve immediately.
*1½ lb. pork loin may be substituted.

Cherry-Cheese Ring
MAKES 12 TO 16 APPETIZER SERVINGS
PREP: 20 MIN., CHILL: 8 HRS.
The cheese mixture may be prepared up to two days ahead and stored in an airtight container in refrigerator.

1 (1-lb.) block sharp Cheddar
  cheese, shredded
1 cup mayonnaise
½ cup chopped onion
¼ tsp. salt
¼ tsp. pepper
¼ to ½ tsp. ground red pepper
1 cup chopped pecans, toasted
1 (12-oz.) jar cherry or strawberry
  preserves
Crackers or bread rounds

1. Beat first 6 ingredients at medium speed with an electric mixer until blended; stir in pecans. Spoon into a lightly greased 5-cup ring mold. Cover and chill 8 hours. Invert mold onto a serving platter, and place a warm damp cloth on ring mold; gently lift mold from cheese mixture.

2. Spoon preserves in center of cheese mixture, and serve immediately with crackers or bread rounds. ▶

Cherry-Cheese Ring

Shrimp Destin

MAKES 4 SERVINGS
PREP: 25 MIN., COOK: 7 MIN.

2 lb. unpeeled, uncooked large fresh shrimp
½ cup butter
⅓ cup chopped green onions
1 Tbsp. minced garlic
¼ cup dry white wine
1 tsp. lemon juice
⅛ tsp. salt
¼ tsp. coarsely ground pepper
1 Tbsp. chopped fresh dill or 1 tsp. dried dillweed
1 Tbsp. chopped fresh parsley
2 (3¼-oz.) French rolls, split lengthwise and toasted
Garnish: fresh parsley sprigs

1. Peel shrimp; devein, if desired.
2. Melt butter in a large skillet over medium heat; sauté onions and garlic 2 minutes or until tender. Add shrimp, wine, and next 3 ingredients. Cook 5 minutes or until shrimp turn pink, stirring occasionally. Stir in dill and parsley.
3. Place toasted roll halves on 4 individual serving plates. Spoon 1 cup shrimp mixture over each roll, and serve immediately. Garnish, if desired.
Note: You can serve Shrimp Destin over hot cooked rice instead of rolls, if desired.

Peppery Peas o' Plenty

MAKES 4 TO 6 SERVINGS
PREP: 15 MIN., COOK: 40 MIN.

4 hickory-smoked bacon slices
1 large onion, chopped
1 cup frozen black-eyed peas
1 cup frozen purple hull peas
1 cup frozen crowder peas
1 cup frozen butter peas
1 cup frozen field peas with snaps
1 (32-oz.) container chicken broth
1 Tbsp. Asian garlic-chili sauce
¾ to 1 tsp. salt
1 Tbsp. freshly ground pepper

1. Cook bacon in Dutch oven until crisp; remove bacon, and drain on paper towels, reserving drippings in pan. Crumble bacon.
2. Sauté chopped onion in hot drippings in Dutch oven over medium-high heat 8 minutes or until translucent. Add 1 cup black-eyed peas and next 8 ingredients, and cook, uncovered, 20 to 25 minutes. Top peas mixture with crumbled bacon.
Note: For testing purposes only, we used Bryan Sweet Hickory Smoked Bacon and A Taste of Thai Garlic Chili Pepper Sauce.

Shrimp Destin

Marmalade-Glazed Beef Patties

MAKES 4 SERVINGS
PREP: 10 MIN., COOK: 25 MIN.

1 lb. ground beef
1 large egg
½ cup fine, dry breadcrumbs
2 Tbsp. prepared horseradish
½ tsp. salt
1 (8-oz.) can water chestnuts, drained and diced
⅔ cup orange marmalade
½ cup water
⅓ cup lite soy sauce
2 Tbsp. lemon juice
1 garlic clove, pressed
Hot cooked rice

1. Combine first 6 ingredients; shape into 4 patties.
2. Cook patties in a large nonstick skillet over medium-high heat 2 minutes on each side or until browned; remove from skillet. Add orange marmalade and next 4 ingredients to skillet. Bring to a boil over medium heat; cook, stirring constantly, 6 minutes. Add patties; reduce heat to low, and simmer 10 minutes. Serve over rice.

Marmalade-Glazed Meatballs:
Shape beef mixture into 1-inch balls; place on a rack in a broiler pan, and broil 5½ inches from heat 5 minutes or until no longer pink; keep warm. Bring marmalade and next 4 ingredients to a boil in a saucepan over medium heat; cook, stirring constantly, 6 minutes. Pour over meatballs. Makes about 3½ dozen. Prep: 25 min., Broil: 5 min., Cook: 6 min.

Garlic-Herb Steaks

MAKES 4 SERVINGS
PREP: 5 MIN., STAND: 30 MIN.,
COOK: 12 MIN.
Use a cast-iron skillet to sear steaks so the garlic crust doesn't fall off.

4 (4-oz.) beef tenderloin fillets
1 tsp. salt
½ tsp. freshly ground pepper
½ tsp. garlic powder
2 Tbsp. chopped fresh parsley
1 Tbsp. minced fresh rosemary
¼ cup olive oil

Chicken Tetrazzini

1. Sprinkle fillets evenly with salt and pepper; coat with garlic powder, parsley, and rosemary. Drizzle oil evenly over steaks. Let stand 30 minutes.
2. Cook steaks in a lightly greased cast-iron grill skillet or in a cast-iron skillet over medium-high heat 4 to 6 minutes on each side or to desired degree of doneness.

Chicken Tetrazzini

MAKES 4 SERVINGS
PREP: 35 MIN., COOK: 20 MIN.,
BAKE: 25 MIN.
To make ahead: Cover and chill before baking. Let stand 30 minutes; uncover and bake 35 minutes or until thoroughly heated.

make ahead

8 oz. spaghetti
3 Tbsp. butter
1 medium onion, chopped
1 green bell pepper, chopped
1 garlic clove, pressed
3 Tbsp. all-purpose flour
2 cups milk
3 cups chopped cooked chicken
1 cup (4 oz.) shredded Cheddar cheese, divided
1 (10¾-oz.) can cream of mushroom soup
¼ cup dry white wine or chicken broth
1 (4-oz.) can sliced mushrooms, drained
1 (2-oz.) jar diced pimiento, drained
2 Tbsp. chopped fresh parsley
1 tsp. salt
½ tsp. pepper

1. Prepare spaghetti according to package directions. Drain.
2. Melt butter in a large skillet over medium heat; add onion, bell pepper, and garlic, and sauté until tender. Stir in flour; cook, stirring constantly, 1 minute. Gradually stir in milk; cook over medium heat, stirring constantly, until thickened and bubbly. Stir in spaghetti, chicken, ¾ cup Cheddar cheese, and next 7 ingredients. Spoon into 4 (2-cup) lightly greased oven-safe bowls.
3. Bake at 350° for 20 minutes; sprinkle with remaining ¼ cup Cheddar cheese, and bake 5 more minutes.
Note: Entire recipe may be baked as directed in a lightly greased 2-qt. baking dish. ◆

Pork Medallions in Mustard Sauce

MAKES 4 SERVINGS
PREP: 15 MIN.,
CHILL: 8 HRS., GRILL: 25 MIN.

make ahead

2 Tbsp. vegetable oil
2 Tbsp. coarse-grained mustard
½ tsp. salt
½ tsp. coarsely ground pepper
1½ lb. pork tenderloin
1 tsp. pepper
Mustard Sauce

1. Stir together first 4 ingredients. Rub mixture over pork, and place in a large zip-top plastic freezer bag. Seal and chill 8 hours; rub pork evenly with 1 tsp. pepper.
2. Grill, covered with grill lid, over medium-high heat (350° to 400°) for 10 minutes; turn meat, and grill 15 more minutes or until a meat thermometer inserted in thickest portion of tenderloin registers 150°. Slice and serve with Mustard Sauce.

Mustard Sauce:

MAKES 1¼ CUPS
PREP: 5 MIN., COOK: 20 MIN.

make ahead

This sauce may also be served with chicken or fish.

1¾ cups whipping cream
¼ cup coarse-grained mustard
¼ tsp. salt
⅛ tsp. ground white pepper

1. Cook whipping cream in a heavy saucepan over medium heat until reduced to 1¼ cups (about 20 minutes). Do not boil. Stir in remaining ingredients, and cook 1 more minute. Store in an airtight container in refrigerator up to 3 days.

Honey Barbecue Chicken

MAKES 8 TO 10 SERVINGS
PREP: 5 MIN.; GRILL: 1 HR., 10 MIN.

Vegetable cooking spray
6 bone-in chicken breasts
8 chicken drumsticks
2 tsp. salt
1 tsp. pepper
Honey Barbecue Sauce

1. Coat cold cooking grate with cooking spray, and place on grill over medium-high heat (350° to 400°). Sprinkle chicken evenly with salt and pepper. Place on food grate.
2. Grill, covered with grill lid, 5 to 10 minutes on each side. Reduce heat to low (under 300°); grill, covered, 40 to 50 minutes for breasts and 30 to 40 minutes for drumsticks or until done. Brush chicken with 1 cup Honey Barbecue Sauce during last 10 minutes of grilling. Serve with remaining 1 cup sauce.

Honey Barbecue Sauce:

MAKES ABOUT 2 CUPS
PREP: 15 MIN., COOK: 10 MIN.

This sauce can be made up to a week in advance.

¼ cup butter
1 medium onion, diced (about 1 cup)
1 cup ketchup
⅓ cup water
¼ cup honey
2 Tbsp. lemon juice
1 Tbsp. Worcestershire sauce
¼ tsp. ground black pepper

1. Melt butter in small saucepan over medium heat; add onion, and sauté 4 to 5 minutes or until tender. Stir in ketchup and remaining ingredients; bring to a boil. Reduce heat, and simmer, uncovered, 5 minutes. Store leftover sauce in an airtight container in refrigerator up to 1 week. ◆

PHOTOGRAPHS: BETH DREILING / STYLING: MINDI SHAPIRO LEVINE / FOOD STYLING: ANGELA SELLERS

Entertaining and Celebrations

Weeknight celebrations, from birthdays to a special dinner with friends, can be a challenge if you don't have a plan. Relax, you have one now. With these foolproof menus and make-ahead appetizers and beverages, you'll easily pull it all off like a pro.

You'll be all set to entertain with these appetizers that can be prepared without much notice. All use convenient pantry and refrigerator staples, and some can be made ahead to keep on hand in the freezer.

At-the-Ready Appetizers

Sesame Chicken Strips

Sesame Chicken Strips
MAKES 8 APPETIZER SERVINGS
PREP: 10 MIN., BAKE: 15 MIN.

2 cups mayonnaise, divided
2 tsp. dried minced onion
2 tsp. dry mustard
1 cup crushed round buttery
  crackers (about 20 crackers)
½ cup sesame seeds
1¾ lb. skinned and boned chicken
  breast tenders
2 Tbsp. honey
2 tsp. prepared mustard

1. Stir together 1 cup mayonnaise, minced onion, and dry mustard in a small bowl. Combine crushed crackers and sesame seeds in a separate bowl.
2. Dip chicken into mayonnaise mixture, and dredge in cracker mixture. Repeat procedure once. Place on a lightly greased rack on an aluminum foil-lined baking sheet.
3. Bake at 425° for 15 minutes or until chicken is done.
4. Stir together remaining 1 cup mayonnaise, honey, and mustard. Serve honey sauce with chicken.

Ginger Dipping Sauce
MAKES ⅓ CUP (ABOUT 5 SERVINGS)
PREP: 10 MIN., COOK: 1 MIN.
Try this tasty sauce with egg rolls or Sesame Chicken Strips.

1 garlic clove, minced
1 Tbsp. minced fresh ginger
1 tsp. dark sesame oil
2 Tbsp. lite soy sauce
1 Tbsp. rice wine vinegar
2 tsp. teriyaki sauce
1 green onion, minced

1. Sauté garlic and ginger in hot oil 1 minute; remove from heat. Whisk in sesame oil, soy sauce, and remaining ingredients.

Caribbean Cashews
MAKES 2 CUPS
PREP: 10 MIN., BAKE: 23 MIN.

make ahead

1½ tsp. butter or margarine
2 cups lightly salted whole
  cashews
2 tsp. grated orange rind
2 tsp. Caribbean Jerk seasoning

1. Preheat oven to 350°. Heat butter in an 8-inch cake pan in oven 2 to 3 minutes or until melted; stir in nuts and remaining ingredients, tossing to coat.
2. Bake at 350° for 20 minutes, stirring occasionally. Arrange cashews in a single layer on wax paper, and let cool. Store in an airtight container.

Stuffed Strawberries

MAKES 1 DOZEN
PREP: 30 MIN.

*Make stuffing and prep
strawberries a day ahead.
Fill strawberries no more than
four hours before serving.*

14 large fresh strawberries, divided
1 (3-oz.) package cream cheese,
   softened
2 Tbsp. finely chopped walnuts or
   pecans
1½ Tbsp. powdered sugar
1 tsp. orange liqueur (optional)

1. Dice 2 strawberries, and set aside.
2. Cut a thin slice from stem end of
each remaining strawberry, forming a
base for strawberries to stand on. Cut
each strawberry into four wedges, starting at pointed end and cutting to, but not
through, stem end.

3. Beat cream cheese at medium speed
with an electric mixer until fluffy. Stir in
diced strawberries, walnuts, powdered
sugar, and, if desired, liqueur. Spoon or
pipe about 1 Tbsp. mixture into each
strawberry.

Sugar-and-Spice Peanuts

MAKES 4 CUPS
PREP: 5 MIN., COOK: 15 MIN.,
BAKE: 30 MIN.

¾ cup sugar
½ cup water
2 cups shelled raw peanuts
1 tsp. pumpkin pie spice

1. Cook sugar and ½ cup water in a
small saucepan over medium heat, stirring occasionally, until sugar dissolves.
Stir in peanuts, and cook 10 minutes or
until sugar starts to crystallize on
peanuts. Sprinkle pumpkin pie spice
evenly over peanuts, stirring to coat.
Spread nuts in a single layer on a lightly greased baking sheet.
2. Bake at 300° for 30 minutes, stirring
every 10 minutes. Cool on baking sheet.
Store in an airtight container.

Spicy Pistachios

MAKES 4 CUPS
PREP: 5 MIN., BAKE: 25 MIN.

*This snack is a homemade version
of the spicy pistachios available in
pricey food catalogs.*

¼ cup Worcestershire sauce
3 Tbsp. butter or margarine, melted
1 tsp. ground chipotle chile pepper
½ tsp. garlic powder
½ tsp. ground cinnamon
4 cups shelled dry-roasted pistachios
   (about 8 cups unshelled)

1. Stir together first 5 ingredients; add
pistachios, tossing to coat. Arrange pistachios in a single layer on a lightly
greased 15- x 10-inch jelly-roll pan.
2. Bake at 350° for 20 to 25 minutes,
stirring after 10 minutes. Arrange in a
single layer on wax paper, and let cool.
Store in an airtight container.
Note: For testing purposes only, we
used McCormick Gourmet Collection
Chipotle Chile Pepper.

Pesto-Goat Cheese Spread

MAKES 3 CUPS
PREP: 15 MIN., CHILL: 2 HRS.

1 (11-oz.) log goat cheese
1 (8-oz.) package cream cheese,
   softened
2 cups loosely packed fresh basil
   leaves
½ cup pine nuts, toasted
3 garlic cloves
2 Tbsp. balsamic vinegar
Toasted pita chips or baguette
   slices

1. Process first 6 ingredients in a food
processor until smooth. Cover and chill
2 hours before serving. Store in an airtight container in refrigerator up to 1
week, or freeze in an airtight container
up to 4 months. Serve with toasted pita
chips or baguette slices. ▶

Stuffed
Strawberries

Tapenade

MAKES 1 CUP
PREP: 10 MIN.

Try this classic olive spread with grilled fish or vegetables on sliced focaccia.

1 (6-oz.) jar pitted kalamata olives, drained
1 anchovy fillet, rinsed
2 garlic cloves, chopped
1 small shallot, chopped
1 tsp. capers
¼ cup olive oil
1 Tbsp. lemon juice
1 Tbsp. chopped fresh parsley
Garnishes: olives, lemon slice, fresh parsley

1. Process first 5 ingredients in a food processor until smooth. With processor running, pour oil through food chute, stopping to scrape down sides. Stir in lemon juice and chopped parsley. Garnish, if desired.

Herbed Feta Spread

MAKES 2½ CUPS
PREP: 10 MIN.

1 (8-oz.) package feta cheese, softened
1 (8-oz.) package cream cheese, softened
3 Tbsp. chopped fresh basil
3 Tbsp. chopped fresh chives
2 Tbsp. olive oil
2 Tbsp. balsamic vinegar
⅓ cup pine nuts, toasted
Garnish: fresh basil sprigs

1. Stir together first 6 ingredients until smooth. Cover and chill up to 1 week. Stir in pine nuts just before serving. Garnish, if desired.

Béarnaise Mayonnaise

MAKES 1 CUP
PREP: 15 MIN., COOK: 5 MIN.

Substitute this for regular mayonnaise on sandwiches.

⅓ cup dry white wine
1 Tbsp. white wine vinegar
2 shallots, minced
1 cup mayonnaise
2 Tbsp. chopped fresh tarragon

(clockwise from top) Tapenade, Herbed Feta Spread, Cucumber-Yogurt Spread, and Béarnaise Mayonnaise

1 tsp. grated lemon rind
⅛ tsp. pepper
Garnish: fresh tarragon sprig

1. Cook first 3 ingredients over medium-high heat 5 minutes or until liquid is reduced to 1 Tbsp. Remove from heat, and cool.
2. Stir together mayonnaise and next 3 ingredients; stir in wine reduction. Cover and chill up to 1 week. Garnish, if desired.

Tomato-Basil Mayonnaise: Stir together 1 cup mayonnaise, 2 Tbsp. tomato paste, and 2 Tbsp. chopped basil until blended.

Gremolata Mayonnaise: Stir together 1 cup mayonnaise, 2 Tbsp. chopped fresh parsley, 2 Tbsp. grated lemon rind, and 1 garlic clove, pressed.

Cucumber-Yogurt Spread

MAKES 2 CUPS
PREP: 15 MIN., CHILL: 24 HRS.

Serve this refreshing spread on soft rolls with grilled chicken, sliced turkey, or fresh tomato slices.

1 (16-oz.) container plain nonfat yogurt
2 small cucumbers, peeled, seeded, and finely chopped
2 garlic cloves, pressed
6 small mint leaves, minced
¼ tsp. salt
¼ tsp. pepper
Garnishes: cucumber slices, fresh mint sprigs

1. Line a mesh strainer with a paper coffee filter. Spoon yogurt into filter, and

Place in a small baking dish.

2. Combine pecans, liqueur, and brown sugar; spread over top of cheese.

3. Bake at 350° for 3 to 5 minutes or just until soft. Serve immediately with apple slices or gingersnaps.

Garlic-and-Dill Feta Cheese Spread
MAKES ABOUT 1 CUP
PREP: 10 MIN., CHILL: 8 HRS.

make ahead

1 (8-oz.) package cream cheese, softened
1 (4-oz.) package crumbled feta cheese

¼ cup mayonnaise
1 garlic clove, minced
1 Tbsp. chopped fresh dill or ½ tsp. dried dillweed
½ tsp. seasoned pepper
¼ tsp. salt
Cucumber slices (optional)

1. Process first 7 ingredients in a food processor until smooth, stopping to scrape down sides. Cover and chill 8 hours. Serve with cucumber slices, if desired.

Note: Spread may be frozen in an airtight container up to 1 month. Thaw in refrigerator at least 24 hours. Stir before serving. ▶

place strainer over a bowl. Cover and chill at least 24 hours.

2. Spoon yogurt into a bowl, discarding liquid (yogurt will have a very thick consistency). Stir in chopped cucumber and next 4 ingredients. Cover and chill up to 3 days. Garnish, if desired.

Coffee-Kissed Pecan Brie
MAKES 8 APPETIZER SERVINGS
PREP: 10 MIN., BAKE: 5 MIN.

1 (13.2-oz.) Brie round
½ cup chopped pecans, toasted
2 Tbsp. coffee-flavored liqueur
1½ Tbsp. brown sugar
Apple slices or gingersnaps

1. Trim rind from top of cheese, leaving a ½-inch border around outside edges.

Coffee-Kissed Pecan Brie

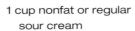
Lemon-Garlic Olives

Marinated Cheese, Olives, and Peppers

MAKES 6 TO 8 APPETIZER SERVINGS
PREP: 15 MIN., CHILL: 1 HR.

make ahead

1½ lb. cubed firm cheeses
   (such as Cheddar, Gouda,
   Havarti, or Monterey Jack)
2 cups olives
1 (7-oz.) jar roasted red
   bell peppers
Cheese Marinade

1. Combine cheeses, olives, and peppers in a large zip-top plastic freezer bag or decorative airtight container. Pour Cheese Marinade over mixture, and chill at least 1 hour or up to 2 days.
Cheese Marinade:
MAKES ABOUT 3 CUPS
PREP: 10 MIN.

1½ cups olive oil
1 cup white balsamic vinegar
¼ cup fresh thyme leaves
2 Tbsp. chopped fresh rosemary
1 tsp. salt
½ tsp. pepper

1. Whisk together all ingredients. Pour into an airtight jar or decorative container. Store in refrigerator up to 1 week.

Lemon-Garlic Olives

MAKES ABOUT 32 APPETIZER
SERVINGS
PREP: 15 MIN., CHILL: 8 HRS.

make ahead

1 (21-oz.) jar pimiento-stuffed
   olives
8 sprigs fresh oregano
6 garlic cloves, pressed
4 lemon slices
20 black peppercorns
6 Tbsp. lemon juice

1. Drain olives, reserving liquid.
2. Layer half each of olives, oregano, garlic, lemon slices, and peppercorns in a 1-qt. jar; repeat layers.
3. Pour 6 Tbsp. lemon juice into jar; add just enough of reserved olive liquid to fill. Replace lid, and chill at least 8 hours. Store in refrigerator up to 2 weeks.

Curry Dip

MAKE 1½ CUPS
PREP: 10 MIN., CHILL: 4 HRS.

make ahead

1 cup nonfat or regular
   sour cream
½ cup fat-free or regular
   mayonnaise
2 Tbsp. minced fresh
   parsley
1 tsp. minced fresh chives
2 Tbsp. grated onion
2 Tbsp. lemon juice
1 tsp. curry powder
2 tsp. prepared mustard
½ tsp. paprika
½ tsp. dried tarragon
Assorted fresh vegetables

1. Stir together first 10 ingredients. Cover and chill at least 4 hours. Serve with assorted fresh vegetables.

Besides serving Curry Dip with veggies, use it as a dressing for chicken salad.

Bacon-Cheese Rounds

Black-eyed Pea Hummus

MAKES 2 CUPS
PREP: 10 MIN., CHILL: 1 HR.

You can find tahini (ground sesame paste) near the peanut butter in most large supermarkets.

1 (15-oz.) can black-eyed peas, rinsed and drained
2 Tbsp. tahini
2 Tbsp. olive oil
¼ cup fresh lemon juice
2 garlic cloves
½ tsp. salt
¼ tsp. ground cumin
½ tsp. freshly ground black pepper
⅛ tsp. ground red pepper
3 Tbsp. water
Olive oil
Garnish: fresh parsley sprig
Pita chips

1. Process first 9 ingredients in a food processor until blended, stopping to scrape down sides. Gradually add 3 Tbsp. water for desired consistency. Cover and chill 1 hour. Drizzle with olive oil, and garnish, if desired. Serve with pita chips.

Traditional Hummus: Substitute 1 (15-oz.) can chickpeas, rinsed and drained, for black-eyed peas. Proceed with recipe as directed. ▶

Bacon-Cheese Rounds

MAKES 8 APPETIZER SERVINGS
PREP: 15 MIN., BAKE: 10 MIN.

1 cup (4 oz.) shredded Swiss cheese
8 bacon slices, cooked and crumbled*
¼ cup mayonnaise
1 tsp. grated onion
½ tsp. celery salt
8 white bread slices
Garnish: chopped fresh chives

1. Stir together first 5 ingredients.
2. Cut each bread slice into 2 (2¼-inch) rounds. Spread 1 heaping Tbsp. cheese mixture on each round. Place on a lightly greased baking sheet.
3. Bake at 325° for 10 minutes. Garnish, if desired.

*1 (2.5-oz.) package fully cooked bacon pieces may be substituted.

Black-eyed Pea Hummus

Green Chile Pimiento
Cheese Tea Sandwiches

Basic Deviled Eggs

MAKES 6 SERVINGS
PREP: 25 MIN.

6 large, hard-cooked eggs,
   peeled
2 Tbsp. mayonnaise
1½ Tbsp. sweet pickle
   relish
1 tsp. prepared mustard
⅛ tsp. salt
Dash of pepper

1. Slice eggs in half lengthwise, and carefully remove yolks. Mash yolks with mayonnaise. Stir in relish, mustard, salt, and pepper. Spoon yolk mixture into egg whites.

Five-Minute Salsa

MAKE 3 CUPS
PREP: 5 MIN.

1 (14.5-oz.) can stewed tomatoes,
   undrained
1 (10-oz.) can diced tomatoes
   and green chiles, undrained
½ to 1 tsp. pepper
½ tsp. garlic salt
Tortilla chips

1. Pulse first 4 ingredients in a blender 30 seconds. Serve with tortilla chips.

Swiss-Onion Dip

MAKES 4 CUPS
PREP: 10 MIN., BAKE: 25 MIN.

1 (10-oz.) package frozen chopped
   onion, thawed
3 cups (12 oz.) shredded Swiss
   cheese
1 cup mayonnaise or salad
   dressing
1 Tbsp. coarse-grained Dijon
   mustard
⅛ tsp. pepper
Melba toast rounds

1. Drain onion on paper towels.
2. Combine onion, cheese, and next 3 ingredients. Spoon mixture into a 1-qt. baking dish.
3. Bake at 325° for 25 minutes or until bubbly and lightly browned. Serve with Melba toast rounds.

Green Chile Pimiento Cheese

MAKES ABOUT 6 CUPS
PREP: 15 MIN.

2 (8-oz.) blocks extra sharp
   Cheddar cheese, shredded
1 (8-oz.) block Monterey Jack
   cheese with peppers, shredded
1 cup mayonnaise
1 (4.5-oz.) can chopped green
   chiles
1 (4-oz.) jar diced pimiento, drained

¼ small sweet onion, minced
2 tsp. Worcestershire sauce

1. Stir together all ingredients in a large bowl.
Green Chile Pimiento Cheese Tea Sandwiches:
Spread ½ cup cheese mixture on each of 6 to 8 bread slices; top with 6 to 8 bread slices. Trim crusts, and cut sandwiches diagonally into quarters or lengthwise into thirds. Reserve remaining cheese mixture for other uses.

Garlic Pepper Jelly

Spicy Chicken Salad With Cabbage Wraps
MAKES 4 TO 6 SERVINGS
PREP: 20 MIN., COOK: 10 MIN.,
CHILL: 15 MIN.

1 lb. skinned and boned chicken
    breasts, cut into large cubes
1½ Tbsp. thinly sliced fresh ginger
½ red onion, thinly sliced
4 green onions, thinly sliced
3½ Tbsp. fish sauce
1 tsp. grated lime rind
¼ cup fresh lime juice
1 small jalapeño pepper, minced
2 tsp. sesame oil
¾ tsp. ground red pepper
½ cup dry-roasted unsalted
    peanuts, coarsely chopped
1 small green cabbage, cut into
    wedges
Toppings: baby carrot slices,
    cucumber slices, radish slices

1. Process chicken in a food processor until the consistency of ground beef.
2. Cook chicken in a lightly greased large skillet over medium-high heat 10 minutes or until done, stirring often. Drain and place in a large bowl.
3. Cut sliced ginger into thin strips. Stir ginger and next 8 ingredients into chicken. Cover and chill at least 15 minutes; stir in peanuts.
4. Spoon chicken salad onto individual cabbage wedges. Serve with desired toppings. ◆

Garlic Pepper Jelly
MAKES 3 CUPS

make ahead

PREP: 5 MIN., COOK: 10 MIN.
Serve over cream cheese or Brie, or use as a basting sauce for chicken or pork.

2 (16-oz.) jars apple jelly
2 Tbsp. dried parsley flakes
1 Tbsp. pressed garlic
½ tsp. dried crushed red pepper
4 tsp. white vinegar

1. Melt apple jelly in a medium saucepan over low heat, stirring often. Stir in parsley and remaining ingredients. Pour into jars or freezer containers; cool. Cover and freeze up to 6 months. (Jelly will not freeze solid.)

pantry items to keep on hand

- black beans
- black-eyed peas
- chickpeas
- diced tomatoes with chiles
- diced green chiles
- mustard
- honey mustard
- olives
- pickled jalapeño peppers (whole and sliced)
- pickled pepperoncini peppers
- apple jelly
- pepper jelly
- salsa
- assorted crackers
- breadcrumbs

Happy Birthday to You

Make a big fuss, and celebrate with family and friends by having a birthday supper during the week. As a rule, the lucky birthday boy or girl gets to pick what will be served—usually their favorite comfort foods. With that in mind, we selected this menu of classics: meatloaf with mashed potatoes and gravy, green beans, and chocolate cake. Best of all, most of the menu can be made ahead.

Herbed Meat Loaf With Sun-dried Tomato Gravy

MAKES 8 SERVINGS
PREP: 15 MIN.; COOK: 5 MIN.;
BAKE: 1 HR., 20 MIN.;
STAND: 10 MIN.

make ahead

Assemble the meatloaf up to 24 hours ahead of time. Cover and chill. Let stand at room temperature 30 minutes before baking.

---

1 cup sun-dried tomatoes, packed in oil (about 24)
1 cup finely chopped onion
½ cup finely chopped green bell pepper
2 garlic cloves, crushed
1 (1-oz.) slice white-wheat bread, torn into small pieces
¼ cup half-and-half
½ cup (2 oz.) shredded Italian cheese blend
¾ tsp. dried basil
¾ tsp. dried oregano
½ tsp. pepper
1 tsp. salt
¼ tsp. dried thyme
1 large egg, lightly beaten
1¾ lb. ultra-lean ground beef
Sun-dried Tomato Gravy

---

1. Drain sun-dried tomatoes well, reserving 1 Tbsp. oil; finely chop tomatoes, and set aside.
2. Sauté onion, bell pepper, and garlic in hot reserved tomato oil in a nonstick skillet over medium-high heat 5 minutes or until tender. Set aside.
3. Place bread in a large bowl. Drizzle half-and-half over bread; toss well to moisten bread. Add reserved tomatoes, onion mixture, cheese, and next 6 ingredients; crumble beef over tomato mixture, and gently combine just until blended. Pack mixture into a lightly greased 9- x 5-inch loaf pan.
4. Bake at 350° for 1 hour and 20 minutes or until meatloaf registers 170°. Let stand in pan 10 minutes. Remove meatloaf from pan. Serve with Sun-dried Tomato Gravy.

Sun-dried Tomato Gravy:
MAKES 1½ CUPS
PREP: 10 MIN., COOK: 10 MIN.

¼ cup sun-dried tomatoes, packed in oil (about 6)

2½ Tbsp. all-purpose flour
1¼ cups milk
¼ cup beef broth
1 Tbsp. finely chopped green
    onions
¼ tsp. salt
¼ tsp. dried basil
⅛ tsp. pepper

1. Drain tomatoes well, and finely chop.
2. Place flour in a small saucepan; gradually add milk, whisking until blended. Stir in tomatoes, broth, and remaining ingredients. Cook over medium heat, whisking constantly, 10 minutes or until thickened.

Basic Mashed Potatoes

MAKES 4 SERVINGS
PREP: 5 MIN., COOK: 15 MIN.

4 medium-size baking potatoes,
    (1½ to 2 lb.)
3 Tbsp. butter, cut up
½ cup milk or half-and-half
¾ tsp. salt
¼ tsp. pepper

1. Peel potatoes, and cut into eighths; cook in boiling water to cover 15 minutes or until tender; drain well. Return potatoes to pan. Add butter, and mash with a potato masher or fork. Stir in milk, salt, and pepper. Mash to achieve desired consistency. Serve hot.

Thyme-Scented Green Beans With Smoked Almonds

make ahead

MAKES 4 SERVINGS
PREP: 15 MIN., COOK: 10 MIN.

Purchase a package of pretrimmed green beans to save time. You can steam green beans, cover, and chill up to 2 days before the celebration.

1 lb. fresh green beans, trimmed
1 Tbsp. butter
1 tsp. dried thyme*
¼ tsp. salt
¼ tsp. pepper
1 Tbsp. chopped smoked almonds*

1. Arrange green beans in a steamer basket over boiling water. Cover and steam 6 minutes or until crisp-tender.
2. Melt butter in a large skillet over medium heat. Stir in green beans, thyme, salt, and pepper; cook until thoroughly heated. Sprinkle beans evenly with almonds.
*1 to 2 Tbsp. chopped fresh thyme may be substituted for dried thyme. 1 Tbsp. chopped toasted almonds may be substituted for smoked almonds.
Note: Smoked almonds may be found in the snack section of the grocery store.

Texas Cake

make ahead

MAKES 24 SERVINGS
PREP: 15 MIN., COOK: 10 MIN.,
BAKE: 25 MIN.
Bake and frost this cake up to 24 hours in advance.

2 cups sugar
2 cups all-purpose flour
1 tsp. baking soda
½ tsp. salt
1 (8-oz.) container sour cream
2 large eggs, lightly beaten
1 cup butter
1 cup water
¼ cup cocoa
Fudge Frosting

1. Combine first 4 ingredients in a large bowl; stir in sour cream and beaten eggs.
2. Melt butter in a heavy saucepan over medium heat. Whisk in 1 cup water and cocoa. Bring to a boil, whisking constantly. Remove from heat. Stir into flour mixture. Pour batter into a lightly greased 15- x 10-inch jelly-roll pan.
3. Bake at 325° for 20 to 25 minutes or until a wooden pick inserted in center of cake comes out clean. Spread Fudge Frosting evenly over warm cake.

Fudge Frosting:

MAKES 3 CUPS
PREP: 20 MIN.

½ cup butter
⅓ cup milk
¼ cup cocoa
1 (1-lb.) package powdered sugar
1 tsp. vanilla extract

1. Melt butter in a saucepan over medium heat. Whisk in milk and cocoa; bring mixture to a boil. Remove from heat. Gradually add powdered sugar, stirring until smooth; stir in vanilla extract.
Note: To thin frosting, add 1 to 2 Tbsp. milk to achieve desired consistency. ◆

Herbed Meat Loaf With Sun-dried Tomato Gravy, Basic Mashed Potatoes, and Thyme-Scented Green Beans With Smoked Almonds

Invite Your Friends to a Delicious Dinner

This classy menu is sure to please.

Impress all your guests with full-of-flavor steaks grilled to perfection, accompanied by sides that rival restaurant selections.

So go ahead, and set the date for a delectable time. Splurge on Prime beef, the freshest produce, and quality ingredients, because there's just nothing else you'll enjoy more than a great meal with your close friends.

Cheesy Green Onion-and-Bacon Mashed Potatoes

MAKES 6 TO 8 SERVINGS
PREP: 15 MIN., COOK: 25 MIN.
Cook and crumble bacon ahead of time to make this dish much faster. You may leave the peels on the potatoes, if you prefer.

4 large baking potatoes, peeled
  and cut into 2-inch pieces
2 cups (8 oz.) shredded colby-
  Jack cheese
6 to 8 bacon slices, cooked and
  crumbled
4 green onions, chopped
2 garlic cloves, pressed
½ cup sour cream
¼ cup butter
1½ tsp. salt
½ tsp. pepper

1. Bring potatoes and water to cover to a boil in a large Dutch oven; cook 25 minutes or until tender. Drain.
2. Mash potatoes with a fork or potato masher; stir in cheese and remaining ingredients. Serve immediately.
To Lighten: Substitute shredded light Mexican cheese blend, reduced-fat bacon, and light sour cream; reduce butter to 2 Tbsp.

Kitchen Express: Substitute 1 (22-oz.) package of frozen mashed potatoes for baking potatoes. Prepare potatoes according to package directions; stir in cheese and remaining ingredients.

Fresh Mozzarella-Tomato-Basil Salad

MAKES 6 TO 8 SERVINGS
PREP: 10 MIN., CHILL: 4 HRS.

½ lb. fresh mozzarella cheese,
  drained
4 large red tomatoes,
  sliced
½ tsp. salt
3 Tbsp. extra virgin
  olive oil
Freshly ground pepper
  to taste
½ cup shredded or chopped
  fresh basil
6 iceberg lettuce leaves (optional)

1. Slice cheese into 12 (¼-inch) slices. Alternate tomato and cheese slices on a platter; sprinkle evenly with salt. Drizzle with olive oil. Cover and chill at least 4 hours. Sprinkle with freshly ground pepper to taste and basil. Serve on lettuce leaves, if desired.

Peppered Rib-eye Steaks

MAKES 6 SERVINGS
PREP: 6 MIN., CHILL: 1 HR.,
GRILL: 16 MIN.
To save time, work on the sides while the steaks chill in the refrigerator.

3 tsp. dried thyme
3 tsp. garlic powder
2 tsp. freshly ground
  black pepper
1½ tsp. salt
1½ tsp. ground red pepper
1½ tsp. lemon pepper
1½ tsp. dried parsley flakes
6 (1½-inch-thick) rib-eye
  steaks
3 Tbsp. olive oil

1. Combine first 7 ingredients. Brush steaks with oil; rub with pepper mixture. Cover and chill 1 hour.
2. Grill, covered with grill lid, over medium-high heat (350° to 400°) 6 to 8 minutes on each side or to desired degree of doneness.

Buttery Garlic Bread

MAKES 8 SLICES
PREP: 10 MIN., COOK: 7 MIN.,
GRILL: 4 MIN.

½ cup butter
4 garlic cloves, pressed
1½ tsp. Italian seasoning
½ tsp. salt
1 (16-oz.) Italian bread loaf

1. Melt butter in a skillet over medium heat. Add garlic, Italian seasoning, and salt; sauté 2 minutes.
2. Cut bread into 1½-inch slices; dip into butter mixture, coating both sides.

3. Grill bread, uncovered, over medium-high heat (350° to 400°) 1 to 2 minutes on each side or until lightly toasted and browned.

Broiled Buttery Garlic Bread: Prepare recipe as directed, coating both sides of bread with butter mixture. Place bread on a baking sheet; broil 5 inches from heat 4 minutes or until toasted. For crispier bread, broil a few minutes longer, checking every minute after 4 minutes.

Marinated Grilled Squash
MAKES 6 SERVINGS
PREP: 15 MIN., CHILL: 1 HR.,
GRILL: 20 MIN.

3 medium-size yellow squash,
   sliced diagonally
3 medium-size zucchini, sliced
   diagonally
⅓ cup olive oil
1 Tbsp. lemon juice
1 garlic clove, pressed
½ tsp. dried marjoram
¼ tsp. salt
¼ tsp. pepper

1. Place yellow squash and zucchini in a heavy-duty zip-top plastic bag.
2. Whisk together oil and next 5 ingredients. Pour over vegetables. Seal and chill 1 hour. Remove vegetables from marinade, reserving marinade.
3. Grill, covered with grill lid, over medium-high heat (350° to 400°) 20 minutes or until crisp-tender, turning and brushing occasionally with reserved marinade.

Turtle Cake
MAKES 12 SERVINGS
PREP: 15 MIN., BAKE: 28 MIN.

1 (18.25-oz.) package German
   chocolate cake mix with pudding
3 cups chopped pecans, divided
¾ cup butter, melted
⅓ cup evaporated milk
1 (14-oz.) package caramels (about
   50 caramels)
½ cup evaporated milk
2 cups (12 oz.) semisweet
   chocolate morsels

Peppered Rib-eye Steaks, Cheesy Green Onion-and-Bacon Mashed Potatoes, Buttery Garlic Bread, Fresh Mozzarella-Tomato-Basil Salad, and Marinated Grilled Squash

1. Combine cake mix, 2 cups pecans, butter, and ⅓ cup evaporated milk in a large bowl; stir until well combined. Reserve half of cake mix mixture for topping. Press remaining half into a greased and floured 13- x 9-inch pan.
2. Bake at 350° for 8 minutes. Remove pan from oven.
3. Microwave caramels and ½ cup evaporated milk in a large microwave-safe bowl at HIGH 2½ to 3 minutes, stirring mixture every 30 seconds until smooth.
4. Sprinkle remaining 1 cup pecans and chocolate morsels evenly over cake. Drizzle caramel mixture over pecans and chocolate morsels. Crumble reserved cake mix mixture evenly over caramel mixture.
5. Bake at 350° for 20 more minutes. Let cool in pan on a wire rack. ◆

This make-ahead spread could not be easier to pull together. All recipes easily double when more than six guests are attending. If playing a game that involves participating at individual tables, plan on preparing one batch of each recipe for each table. For example, with four tables, make each recipe four times. The appetizer serves 18, so you shouldn't have to double it. Just divide the cheese mixture in smaller portions, if needed.

Girls' Game Night

Cinnamon-Chocolate Chip Ice-cream Balls

Chocolate Martinis

Chocolate Martinis
MAKES 10 TO 12 SERVINGS
PREP: 3 MIN., CHILL: 1 HR.,
STAND: 5 MIN.
Start the party off right with this sweet and simple concoction.

make ahead

2 to 2½ cups vodka, chilled
1¼ cups chocolate liqueur
¼ cup raspberry liqueur
¼ cup half-and-half (optional)
Chocolate liqueur or syrup
Sweetened cocoa

1. Stir together vodka, liqueurs, and, if desired, half-and-half in a large pitcher; chill at least 1 hour.
2. Fill glasses with ice. Let stand 5 minutes; discard ice.
3. Coat rims of chilled glasses with chocolate liqueur; dip in cocoa, coating rims. Pour vodka mixture into glasses. Serve immediately.
Note: For testing purposes only, we used Godiva Original Chocolate Liqueur for chocolate liqueur, Chambord for raspberry liqueur, and Ghirardelli Sweet Ground Chocolate and Cocoa for sweetened cocoa.
Individual Chocolate Martini: Combine ¼ cup vodka, 2 Tbsp. chocolate liqueur, 1½ tsp. raspberry liqueur, 6 ice cubes, and, if desired, a dash of half-and-half in a martini shaker. Cover with lid, and shake until thoroughly chilled. Remove lid, and strain into a chilled glass. Serve immediately. Makes 1 serving.

Slow-cooker Fajitas

MAKES 4 TO 6 SERVINGS
PREP: 12 MIN., COOK: 10 HRS.

Buy enough steak for your party when it is on sale at the grocery store. If you're serving a crowd, cook and freeze 1 recipe each day, or borrow a few slow cookers from your neighbors.

1½ lb. flank steak, cut into 4 to 6 pieces
1 medium onion, chopped
1 green bell pepper, sliced
1 jalapeño pepper, seeded and chopped
2 garlic cloves, pressed
1 Tbsp. chopped fresh cilantro
1 tsp. chili powder
1 tsp. ground cumin
1 tsp. ground coriander
¾ to 1 tsp. salt
1 (10-oz.) can diced tomatoes and green chiles, drained
Flour tortillas

Toppings: shredded Cheddar cheese, sour cream, salsa
Garnish: cilantro sprigs

1. Place steak in a 5-qt. slow cooker; top with onion and next 9 ingredients.
2. Cover and cook on HIGH 5 hours or on LOW 10 hours. Remove meat, and shred with 2 forks. Serve with tortillas and desired toppings. Garnish, if desired.
Note: To freeze after cooking: Before shredding meat, reserve at least 1 cup of drippings, if desired, and shred with 2 forks. Place shredded meat and drippings in a large zip-top plastic freezer bag. Seal and freeze up to 1 month. Thaw in refrigerator, and thoroughly heat before serving.

Smoky Green Chile Cheddar Cheese With Avocado-Mango Salsa

MAKES 18 SERVINGS
PREP: 40 MIN., CHILL: 8 HRS.

2 (8-oz.) packages cream cheese, softened
2 (8-oz.) blocks Monterey Jack cheese with peppers, shredded
1 (16-oz.) block smoked Cheddar cheese, shredded
6 green onions, minced
2 (4.5-oz.) cans chopped green chiles, drained
1 (1¼-oz.) envelope taco seasoning mix
Avocado-Mango Salsa
Crackers or tortilla chips

1. Combine first 6 ingredients in a large bowl. Divide mixture into 2 equal por-

Smoky Green Chile Cheddar Cheese with Avocado-Mango Salsa

tions. Shape each into a 6-inch round. Cover and chill 8 hours, or freeze up to 1 month; thaw in the refrigerator 8 hours.
2. Place cheese rounds on serving plates; top evenly with Avocado-Mango Salsa. Serve with tortilla chips.
Note: Smoked Cheddar cheese may be found in the deli section of your grocery store. Cheese mixture may be divided into 4 portions and pressed into 4 lightly greased ramekins, if desired. Freeze and thaw as directed. Invert cheese mixture onto serving plates.

Avocado-Mango Salsa:
MAKES ABOUT 5 CUPS
PREP: 20 MIN., CHILL: 8 HRS.

¼ cup hot jalapeño jelly
¼ cup fresh lime juice
2 large mangoes, peeled and diced*
2 large avocados, diced
1 large red bell pepper, diced
¼ cup chopped fresh cilantro

1. Whisk together jelly and lime juice in a large bowl. Stir in remaining ingredients until blended. Cover and chill 8 hours.
*1 (26-oz.) jar refrigerated mango pieces, drained, may be substituted.

Cinnamon-Chocolate Chip Ice-cream Balls

MAKES 6 SERVINGS
PREP: 25 MIN., FREEZE: 2 HRS.

We used vanilla ice cream for this delicious dessert. You can substitute your favorite flavor.

1½ cups cinnamon-sugar whole wheat-and-rice cereal, crushed
½ cup semisweet chocolate mini-morsels
1 cup finely chopped pecans (optional)
1 qt. ice cream
Caramel syrup

1. Combine crushed cereal, morsels, and, if desired, pecans in a large bowl.
2. Scoop out ice cream, and shape into 6 (2½-inch) balls. Roll balls in cereal mixture, coating evenly. Place in a 9-inch square pan; freeze at least 2 hours or until firm. Drizzle with caramel syrup before serving.
Note: For testing purposes only, we used Cinnamon Toast Crunch cereal. ◆

Slow-cooker Fajitas

PHOTOGRAPHS: BETH DREILING / STYLING: MINDI SHAPIRO LEVINE / FOOD STYLING: ANGELA SELLERS

Come Over for Drinks

Try new liquid refreshments for a change of pace from everyday thirst quenchers. Stir up lemonade, blend a margarita, or mix up some hot chocolate to enjoy now, or make it ahead for a celebration.

Raspberry Lemonade, Kiwi-Lemonade Spritzer, and Fresh Mint-Citrus Sipper

Raspberry Lemonade
MAKES ABOUT 6 CUPS
PREP: 10 MIN.

1 (14-oz.) package frozen raspberries, thawed
1 (16-oz.) jar maraschino cherries without stems
1¼ cups sugar
¾ cup fresh lemon juice (about 5 lemons)
¼ cup fresh lime juice (about 1 large lime)
3 cups water

1. Process first 5 ingredients in a blender until smooth, stopping to scrape down sides. Pour fruit mixture through a wire-mesh strainer into a pitcher, discarding solids. Stir in 3 cups water. Serve over ice.

Blackberry Lemonade: Substitute 1 (14-oz.) package frozen blackberries, thawed, for frozen raspberries. Proceed as directed. Makes 6 cups.

Cherry-Berry Lemonade: Substitute 1 (16-oz.) package frozen mixed berries, thawed, for frozen raspberries. Proceed as directed, using 2 cups water. Makes 5 cups.

Cherry-Berry Lemonade Pops: Pour Cherry-Berry Lemonade evenly into 14 (4-oz.) plastic pop molds. Insert plastic pop sticks, and freeze 4 hours or until firm. Makes 14 pops.

Kiwi-Lemonade Spritzer
MAKES 5 CUPS
PREP: 10 MIN.

4 kiwifruit, peeled
1 (12-oz.) can frozen lemonade concentrate, undiluted and thawed
3 cups lemon-lime soft drink, chilled

1. Cut kiwifruit into chunks. Process fruit chunks and lemonade concentrate in a food processor until smooth, stopping to scrape down sides. Pour mixture through a wire-mesh strainer into a pitcher, discarding solids. Stir in lemon-lime soft drink just before serving.

Strawberry-Kiwi-Lemonade Spritzer: Process 2 cups fresh strawberries; 4 kiwifruit, peeled and cut into chunks; and 1 (12-oz.) can frozen lemonade concentrate, undiluted and thawed, in a food processor until smooth, stopping to scrape down sides. Proceed as directed. Makes 7 cups.

Blue Margaritas
MAKES ABOUT 5 CUPS
PREP: 5 MIN.

1 (10-oz.) can frozen margarita mix
¾ cup tequila
¼ cup blue curaçao liqueur
2 Tbsp. lime juice

1. Combine all ingredients in a blender. Fill with ice to 5-cup level, and process until smooth. Serve immediately.

Hot Chocolate Mix
MAKES 14 SERVINGS
PREP: 5 MIN.
 make ahead

1 (9.6-oz.) package nonfat dry milk
4 cups miniature marshmallows
1½ cups powdered sugar
1 cup unsweetened cocoa

1. Stir together all ingredients in a large bowl. Store chocolate mixture in an airtight container at room temperature.
Hot Chocolate: Stir ½ cup Hot Chocolate Mix into 1 cup hot milk. Serve immediately. Makes 1 serving. Prep: 5 min.

Fruit Punch
MAKES 12 CUPS
PREP: 5 MIN.
 make ahead

This recipe can be prepared with or without the rum. Make a batch of each, pour into pitchers, and tie a ribbon on one to distinguish between the two.

3 cups cranberry juice cocktail
2 cups pineapple juice
2 cups orange juice
1 (1-liter) bottle ginger ale, chilled
¾ to 1 cup light rum (optional)
Garnish: 1 star fruit, cut into
    ¼-inch slices

1. Combine first 3 ingredients in a large bowl, and chill up to 8 hours, if desired. Stir ginger ale and, if desired, rum into juice mixture just before serving. Serve over ice; garnish, if desired.

Coffee Ice-cream Punch
MAKES ABOUT 13 CUPS
PREP: 20 MIN.

1 qt. chilled Coffee
    Concentrate*
1 cup whipping cream
½ tsp. almond extract
Dash of salt
1 qt. vanilla ice cream
1 qt. chocolate ice cream

1. Whisk together 1 qt. Coffee Concentrate and next 3 ingredients. Scoop vanilla and chocolate ice creams into a punch bowl; add Coffee Concentrate mixture, gently stirring until ice cream slightly melts. Serve punch in glass mugs.
*1 qt. strong brewed coffee may be substituted for Coffee Concentrate.

Coffee Concentrate:
MAKES ABOUT 3 QT.
PREP: 30 MIN., STAND: 12 HRS.
make ahead
Use this recipe, adapted from Commander's Kitchen cookbook; it will last up to one month in the refrigerator.

1 lb. ground coffee with
    chicory or dark roast
    ground coffee
3½ qt. cold water

1. Stir together ground coffee and 3½ qt. cold water in a 1-gal. pitcher until all ground coffee is wet; let stand 12 hours at room temperature.
2. Pour coffee mixture through a large, fine wire-mesh strainer, discarding grounds. Clean strainer; place a coffee filter or double layer of cheesecloth in strainer, and pour coffee mixture through lined strainer. Return Coffee Concentrate mixture to pitcher; cover and chill up to 1 month.
Note: To make iced coffee, stir together ¼ cup each of Coffee Concentrate and water. If desired, stir in milk and sugar. Serve over ice.

Fresh Mint-Citrus Sipper
MAKES 8 CUPS
PREP: 15 MIN.

1½ cups fresh lemon juice
1 cup fresh lime juice
1 cup fresh orange juice
Fresh Mint Sugar Syrup
1 (25-oz.) bottle lemon-flavored
    sparkling water, chilled (about
    3 cups)

1. Combine first 4 ingredients in a large pitcher, stirring well. Stir in sparkling water just before serving. Serve over ice.
Fresh Mint Sugar Syrup:
MAKES 2 CUPS
PREP: 5 MIN., COOK: 5 MIN. make ahead
You can store this sugar syrup in an airtight container in the refrigerator up to two weeks.

2 cups sugar
1 cup water
1 cup loosely packed fresh
    mint leaves

1. Bring all ingredients to a boil in a saucepan, stirring until sugar dissolves; boil 1 minute. Remove mixture from heat, and cool.
2. Pour mixture through a wire-mesh strainer into a pitcher, discarding mint leaves.
Fresh Mint-Citrus Sipper by the Glass: Combine 3 Tbsp. Fresh Mint Sugar Syrup; 2 Tbsp. each fresh lemon, lime, and orange juices; and ¾ cup lemon-flavored sparkling water, chilled; stir mixture well. ◆

Decorative Touches

Use these simple ideas to complement the great food at your next party.

When you aren't serving them for dinner, bell peppers make stylish containers for cut flowers.

Painted wooden letters in assorted sizes from a crafts store offer many options for a display.

Tie flatware and a bloom with sheer ribbon for an elegant look.

Small, simple arrangements provide a nice contrast to main centerpieces.

Fresh herbs and cut flowers tucked into a plastic wrap-lined colander dress up a kitchen counter or island.

To save money, use greenery from your yard, and purchase just a few blooms from the grocery.

A footed cake stand makes a nice base for a pillar candle. Use fresh fruit and greenery as finishing touches.

PHOTOGRAPHS: JEAN ALLSOPP, TINA CORNETT, BETH DREILING, LAUREY W. GLENN / STYLING: LISA POWELL BAILEY, BUFFY HARGETT

Last-Minute Goodies

These easy-to-prepare and delicious recipes will come to the rescue when you forget you volunteered to bake cupcakes or you didn't see the reminder for the bake sale. Maybe you get a short-notice call to bring a treat for an office party. Save the more complicated desserts for other occasions when you have more time. These sweets will do just fine in a pinch.

Quick Italian Cream Cakes

Cakes and Cupcakes

Bake these confections to take to school, the office, or a special event.

Most of these cakes and cupcakes start with basic mixes to ease preparation, but we dressed them up for tastes-like-scratch flavor. Short on time? Purchase cupcakes from the grocery store, and decorate them using our simple instructions. Take your creative confections to your next gathering.

Quick Italian Cream Cakes

MAKES 4 MINI LOAF CAKES
PREP: 10 MIN., BAKE: 35 MIN.,
CHILL: 2 HRS.

make ahead

Whether in loaf pans or as a layer cake, the result is traditional flavor in about half the time.

1 (18.5-oz.) package white cake mix with pudding
3 large eggs
1¼ cups buttermilk
¼ cup vegetable oil
1 (3½-oz.) can sweetened flaked coconut
⅔ cup chopped pecans, toasted
Cream Cheese Frosting

1. Beat first 4 ingredients at medium speed with an electric mixer 2 minutes. Stir in coconut and pecans. Pour into 4 greased and floured 5¾- x 3¼-inch miniature disposable loaf pans.

2. Bake at 350° for 33 to 35 minutes or until a wooden pick inserted in center comes out clean. Cool in pans on wire racks 10 minutes. Remove from pans, and cool completely on wire racks.

3. Spread Cream Cheese Frosting on top of cakes. Cover and chill 2 hours before slicing.

Cream Cheese Frosting:
MAKES 4 CUPS
PREP: 10 MIN.

1 (8-oz.) package cream cheese, softened
½ cup butter, softened ▶

6 cups powdered sugar

1 tsp. vanilla extract

1. Beat cream cheese and butter at medium speed with an electric mixer until creamy; gradually add sugar, beating well. Stir in vanilla.

Quick Italian Cream Layer Cake: Pour batter into 3 greased and floured 9-inch round cake pans. Bake at 350° for 15 to 17 minutes or until a wooden pick inserted in center comes out clean. Cool in pans on wire racks 10 minutes. Remove from pans, and cool completely on wire racks. Spread Cream Cheese Frosting between layers and on top and sides of cake. Cover and chill 2 hours before slicing. Prep: 10 min., Bake: 17 min., Chill: 2 hrs.

German Chocolate Snack Cake

MAKES 18 SQUARES
PREP: 15 MIN., BAKE: 1 HR.

1 (18.25-oz.) package German
   chocolate cake mix

4 large eggs, divided

½ cup chopped pecans, toasted

½ cup butter or margarine, melted

1 (16-oz.) package powdered sugar

1 (8-oz.) package cream cheese,
   softened

Ice cream or whipped topping

1. Stir together cake mix, 1 egg, pecans, and butter; press mixture into bottom of a lightly greased 13- x 9-inch pan.

2. Beat powdered sugar, cream cheese, and remaining 3 eggs at medium speed with an electric mixer until creamy. Spoon powdered sugar mixture over batter in pan.

3. Bake at 300° for 1 hour. Cool and cut into 2½- to 3-inch squares. Serve with ice cream.

Mississippi Mud Cake

MAKES 15 SERVINGS
PREP: 20 MIN., BAKE: 30 MIN.

1 cup butter, melted

2 cups sugar

½ cup unsweetened cocoa

4 large eggs, lightly beaten

1 tsp. vanilla extract

Mississippi Mud Cake

⅛ tsp. salt

1½ cups all-purpose flour

1½ cups coarsely chopped pecans,
   toasted

1 (10.5-oz.) bag miniature
   marshmallows

Chocolate Frosting

1. Whisk together melted butter and next 5 ingredients in a large bowl. Stir in flour and chopped pecans. Pour batter into a greased and floured 15- x 10-inch jelly-roll pan.

2. Bake at 350° for 20 to 25 minutes or until a wooden pick inserted in center comes out clean. Remove from oven; top warm cake evenly with marshmallows. Return to oven, and bake 5 more minutes. Drizzle Chocolate Frosting over warm cake. Cool completely.

Note: Two (19.5-oz.) packages brownie mix, prepared according to package directions, may be substituted for first 7 ingredients. Stir in chopped pecans. Bake at 350° for 30 minutes. Proceed with marshmallows and Chocolate Frosting as directed.

Chocolate Frosting:
MAKES 2 CUPS
PREP: 10 MIN.

1 (16-oz.) package powdered
   sugar, sifted

½ cup milk

¼ cup butter, softened

⅓ cup unsweetened
   cocoa

1. Beat all ingredients at medium speed with an electric mixer until smooth.

Lemonade Cupcakes

MAKES 30 CUPCAKES
PREP: 15 MIN., BAKE: 22 MIN.

Tint cream cheese frosting with blue food coloring to create water for chewy candy fish.

1 (6-oz.) can frozen lemonade
   concentrate, thawed
1 (18.25-oz.) package white
   cake mix
1 (8-oz.) carton sour cream
1 (3-oz.) package cream cheese,
   softened
3 large eggs
1 (16-oz.) can cream cheese
   frosting
Garnishes: chewy candies,
   candy sprinkles

1. Remove 2 Tbsp. lemonade concentrate from can, and reserve for another use.
2. Combine remaining concentrate, cake mix, and next 3 ingredients in a mixing bowl. Beat at low speed with an electric mixer until moistened. Beat at high speed 3 minutes, stopping to scrape down sides. Spoon batter into 30 paper-lined muffin cups, filling each three-fourths full.
3. Bake at 350° for 18 to 22 minutes or until a wooden pick inserted in center comes out clean. Cool in pans on wire racks 5 minutes. Remove cupcakes from pans; cool completely on wire racks. Spread evenly with frosting. Garnish, if desired.

Lemonade Cupcakes

Piglet Cupcakes

MAKES 30 CUPCAKES
PREP: 30 MIN., BAKE: 25 MIN.

Any flavor cake mix will work with this recipe.

1 (18.25-oz.) package
   chocolate cake mix with
   pudding
2 (12-oz.) containers pink
   ready-to-spread frosting

15 large marshmallows, halved
120 miniature chocolate morsels
60 miniature marshmallows
120 pink jelly beans

1. Prepare cake mix according to package directions. Spoon batter into paper- or foil-lined muffin cups, filling two-thirds full; bake according to package directions. Cool completely on wire racks. Spread cupcakes evenly with ready-to-spread frosting.
2. Position 1 large marshmallow half, resembling a snout, on each cupcake. Press 2 chocolate morsels, flat sides up, in center of snout.
3. Press 1 chocolate morsel, flat side up, into each miniature marshmallow to create eyes; position 2 marshmallow eyes on each cupcake.
4. Position 2 jelly beans above each eye for ears.

Piglet Cupcakes

Spider Cupcakes

MAKES 30 CUPCAKES
PREP: 30 MIN., BAKE: 25 MIN.

1 (18.25-oz.) package white
   cake mix
2 (12-oz.) containers
   chocolate ready-to-
   spread frosting
30 large malted milk balls
60 red cinnamon
   candies
1 (1¼-oz.) package
   red or black string
   licorice

1. Prepare and bake cake mix according to package directions for cupcakes. Cool completely; spread frosting on top of cupcakes.
2. Fill a piping bag or sandwich-size zip-top plastic bag with remaining frosting. (Snip a small hole in 1 corner of zip-top plastic bag.) Pipe a small frosting mound in the center of each cupcake. Press malted milk

Spider Cupcakes

balls into each frosting mound for body; add 2 cinnamon candies to each cupcake for eyes.
3. Cut licorice into 240 (2- to 3-inch long) strips. Insert 4 strips into each side of frosting mound for legs.
Octopus Cupcakes: Substitute desired color frosting for chocolate frosting. Substitute desired color gum balls for malted milk balls. Substitute desired color string licorice for red or black string licorice. Proceed as directed.

Cupcake Surprises

MAKES 2 DOZEN
PREP: 20 MIN., BAKE: 22 MIN.

1 (18.25-oz.) package Swiss
   chocolate cake mix
2 (3-oz.) packages cream cheese,
   softened
½ cup sugar
1 large egg, lightly beaten
1 (6-oz.) package milk chocolate
   morsels
¼ cup sweetened flaked coconut

1. Prepare cake mix according to package directions; set batter aside.
2. Stir together cream cheese, sugar, and egg. Stir in milk chocolate morsels and coconut.
3. Spoon cake batter evenly into 24 paper-lined muffin cups, filling each half full. Drop cream cheese mixture by rounded teaspoonfuls evenly into center of cupcakes.
4. Bake at 350° for 19 to 22 minutes or until a wooden pick inserted in center comes out clean. Cool cupcakes in pans on a wire rack for 15 minutes. Remove cupcakes from pans, and cool completely on wire racks. ▶

Tropical Dump Cake

MAKES 8 TO 10 SERVINGS
PREP: 10 MIN., BAKE: 50 MIN.

2 (20-oz.) cans crushed pineapple,
   undrained
1 (18.25-oz.) package white cake mix
½ cup butter or margarine, cut up
2 cups pecans, toasted
Ice cream or whipped topping

1. Drain 1 can crushed pineapple.
Spread both the drained and undrained
pineapple on bottom of a lightly greased
13- x 9-inch pan. Sprinkle cake mix
over fruit. Dot evenly with butter; sprinkle with pecans.
2. Bake at 350° for 45 to 50 minutes
or until golden and bubbly. Serve with
ice cream.

Birthday Party Brownie Cakes

MAKES 12 SERVINGS
PREP: 10 MIN., BAKE: 30 MIN.

make ahead

1 (21-oz.) package brownie mix
½ cup vegetable oil
¼ cup cranberry juice
2 large eggs
Toppings: semisweet chocolate
   morsels, candy-coated
   chocolate pieces, chopped
   pecans, candy sprinkles

1. Stir together first 4 ingredients until
smooth. Spoon batter into 12 lightly
greased muffin cups. Sprinkle with
desired toppings.
2. Bake at 375° for 30 minutes or until
a wooden pick inserted in center comes
out clean. Remove from pan, and cool
on a wire rack.

Apple-Blueberry Crunch

MAKES 8 TO 10 SERVINGS
PREP: 10 MIN., BAKE: 50 MIN.

1 (21-oz.) can apple pie filling
1 (14-oz.) package frozen blueberries
1 cup sugar
1 (18.25-oz.) package white cake mix
½ cup butter or margarine, melted
1 cup chopped walnuts, toasted
Ice cream or whipped topping

Tropical Dump Cake

1. Spread apple pie filling on bottom of
a lightly greased 13- x 9-inch pan.
2. Toss together frozen blueberries and
¾ cup sugar, and spoon over apple pie
filling. Sprinkle cake mix evenly over
fruit, and drizzle with melted butter.
Sprinkle with chopped walnuts and
remaining ¼ cup sugar.
3. Bake at 350° for 45 to 50 minutes
or until golden and bubbly. Serve with
ice cream.

Mini Poppy Seed-Lemon Cakes

MAKES ABOUT 2 DOZEN
PREP: 5 MIN., BAKE: 20 MIN.

1 (18.5-oz.) package yellow cake
   mix with pudding
⅔ cup vegetable oil
⅔ cup apricot nectar
4 large eggs
⅓ cup poppy seeds
½ tsp. grated lemon rind
2½ Tbsp. fresh lemon juice

1. Combine all ingredients, stirring

until blended. Spoon into greased muffin
pans, filling two-thirds full.
2. Bake at 400° for 18 to 20 minutes or
until golden brown. Remove from pans
immediately, and cool on wire racks.

Cherry-Pineapple Dump Cake

MAKES 8 TO 10 SERVINGS
PREP: 10 MIN., BAKE: 1 HR.

1 (20-oz.) can crushed pineapple,
   undrained
1 (21-oz.) can cherry pie filling
1 (18.25-oz.) package yellow cake mix
¾ cup butter or margarine, melted
½ cup chopped pecans, toasted
Ice cream or whipped topping

1. Spread crushed pineapple on bottom
of a lightly greased 13- x 9-inch pan. Top
pineapple with cherry pie filling, and
sprinkle cake mix evenly over fruit. Drizzle with melted butter, and sprinkle with
chopped pecans.
2. Bake at 350° for 50 to 60 minutes or until golden and bubbly. Serve with ice cream.

Ooey-Gooey Butter Cake

MAKES 12 TO 15 SERVINGS
PREP: 15 MIN., BAKE: 40 MIN.

1 (16-oz.) package pound cake mix
½ cup butter or margarine, melted
4 large eggs, divided
1 (8-oz.) package cream cheese,
   softened
1¼ cups powdered sugar, divided
1 cup chopped pecans
1 cup (6 oz.) semisweet chocolate
   morsels

1. Beat cake mix, butter, and 2 eggs at medium speed with an electric mixer until smooth. Pour batter into a lightly greased 13- x 9-inch pan.
2. Beat remaining 2 eggs, cream cheese, and 1 cup powdered sugar at medium speed until smooth. Pour over cake batter. Sprinkle evenly with pecans and chocolate morsels.
3. Bake at 350° for 30 to 40 minutes or until a wooden pick inserted in center comes out clean. Cool in pan on a wire rack. Sprinkle cake evenly with remaining ¼ cup powdered sugar.

Oatmeal Cake

MAKES 12 TO 15 SERVINGS
PREP: 30 MIN., STAND: 20 MIN.,
BAKE: 30 MIN., BROIL: 3 MIN.

1½ cups boiling water
1 cup uncooked regular oats
½ cup butter, softened
1 cup sugar
2½ cups firmly packed brown
   sugar, divided
1 tsp. ground cinnamon
¼ tsp. ground nutmeg
1 tsp. vanilla extract
2 large eggs
1½ cups all-purpose flour
1 tsp. baking soda
½ tsp. salt
1½ to 2 cups sweetened flaked
   coconut
1½ cups chopped pecans
⅓ cup butter or margarine,
   melted
⅓ cup milk
Garnish: whipped topping

1. Stir together 1½ cups boiling water and oats; let stand 20 minutes.

2. Beat ½ cup butter, 1 cup sugar, and 1 cup brown sugar in a large bowl at medium speed with an electric mixer until creamy; add cinnamon and next 3 ingredients, beating well.
3. Stir in flour, baking soda, and salt just until moistened; beat in oatmeal mixture. Pour batter into a lightly greased 13- x 9-inch pan.
4. Bake at 350° for 30 minutes or until a wooden pick inserted in center comes out clean.
5. Combine remaining 1½ cups brown sugar, coconut, and remaining ingredients in a bowl; spread over warm cake. Broil 8 inches from heat 2 to 3 minutes or until golden. Garnish with whipped topping, if desired.

Two-Layer Oatmeal Cake: Bake cake as directed; let stand in pan on wire rack 10 minutes. Remove from pan, and let cool completely on wire rack. Place cake on a baking sheet. Prepare topping, and spread evenly over top of cake. Broil as directed. Let cool completely, and cut in half, forming 2 (6½- x 9-inch) rectangles. Stack layers, topping sides up.

Black Forest Crisp

MAKES 8 TO 10 SERVINGS
PREP: 15 MIN., BAKE: 50 MIN.

This is our own one-pan interpretation of the attractive Black Forest torte.

1 (21-oz.) can cherry pie filling
1 (8¼-oz.) can crushed pineapple,
   undrained
½ cup slivered almonds, toasted
1 cup semisweet chocolate
   morsels
1 cup sweetened flaked coconut
1 (18.25-oz.) package devil's food
   cake mix
½ cup butter or margarine, cut up
Ice cream or whipped topping

1. Layer cherry pie filling, crushed pineapple, slivered almonds, chocolate morsels, and flaked coconut in a lightly greased 13- x 9-inch baking dish. Sprinkle cake mix over layers, and dot evenly with butter.
2. Bake at 350° for 45 to 50 minutes or until golden and bubbly. Serve with ice cream. ◆

Oatmeal Cake

last-minute goodies

A handful of salty, seasoned crackers ranks high on our list for a tasty treat. So do sweet little morsels you can pop in your mouth for bite-size desserts. Get your snack groove going with these delicious choices.

Snack Crackers

MAKES 6 CUPS
PREP: 5 MIN., BAKE: 15 MIN.

make ahead

½ cup vegetable oil
1 (1-oz.) envelope Ranch dressing
    mix
1 (10-oz.) package oyster crackers
½ (10-oz.) package bite-size
    Cheddar cheese crackers (2 cups)

---

1. Whisk together oil and dressing mix in a large bowl; add crackers, tossing to coat. Spread mixture in a single layer on a lightly greased baking sheet.
2. Bake at 350° for 15 minutes, stirring after 7 minutes. Let cool in a single layer on wax paper. Store in an airtight container.

Snacks and Bites

These nibbles satisfy both a sweet tooth and a salty snack craving.

Snack Crackers

Peanut Butter Fudge

MAKES 1¾ LB.
PREP: 10 MIN., COOK: 5 MIN.

⅔ cup evaporated milk
1⅔ cups sugar
½ tsp. salt
1½ cups miniature marshmallows
1 (10-oz.) package peanut butter
    morsels
½ cup chopped peanuts
1 tsp. vanilla extract

---

1. Bring first 3 ingredients to a boil in a large saucepan. Cook over medium heat, stirring constantly, 5 minutes; remove from heat. Add remaining ingredients; stir until smooth. Pour into a greased 9-inch square pan; cool. Cut into squares.

Orange-Nut Balls

MAKES 5 DOZEN
PREP: 30 MIN., CHILL: 1 HR.

make ahead

½ cup butter or margarine, melted
1 (16-oz.) package powdered
    sugar, sifted
1 (6-oz.) can frozen orange juice
    concentrate, thawed
1 (12-oz.) package vanilla wafers,
    crushed
1 cup finely chopped pecans
1 (14-oz.) package sweetened
    flaked coconut

---

1. Stir together first 5 ingredients. Form into 1-inch balls; roll in coconut. Cover and chill 1 hour or until firm. Store in refrigerator up to 3 weeks.

White Chocolate-Peanut Butter Crunch

MAKES 1¾ LB.
PREP: 15 MIN., STAND: 15 MIN.

---

8 (2-oz.) vanilla bark coating squares
2 Tbsp. creamy peanut butter
2 cups miniature marshmallows
2 cups crisp rice cereal
2 cups dry-roasted peanuts

---

1. Microwave coating squares in a large microwave-safe bowl at HIGH 2 minutes or until melted, stirring every 30 seconds. Stir in peanut butter until smooth. Stir in marshmallows, cereal, and peanuts.
2. Drop by teaspoonfuls onto wax paper. Let stand 15 minutes or until firm.

PHOTOGRAPHS: BETH DREILING, JOHN O'HAGAN / STYLING: MINDI SHAPIRO LEVINE / FOOD STYLING: LYDA JONES BURNETTE

Starry Snack Mix

Butterscotch Drops

MAKES 2½ DOZEN

PREP: 15 MIN.

These bite-size beauties are perfect with a cup of coffee in the afternoon.

1 (6-oz.) package butterscotch morsels*
1 cup dry-roasted peanuts
1 cup shoestring potato sticks, broken into pieces

1. Melt morsels in a saucepan over low heat. Stir in peanuts and potato sticks. Drop by teaspoonfuls onto wax paper, and cool completely.

*1 (6-oz.) package peanut butter morsels may be substituted.

Butterscotch Drops

Starry Snack Mix

MAKES 18 CUPS

PREP: 5 MIN.

make ahead

Package this mix in cellophane bags for portable treats or party favors.

2 (8-oz.) packages crispy cereal squares snack mix
1 (15-oz.) package raisins
1 (12-oz.) jar honey-roasted peanuts
1 (11-oz.) package fish-shaped Cheddar cheese crackers

1. Combine all ingredients. Store in an airtight container.

Note: For testing purposes only, we used Chex Mix Bold Party Blend for crispy cereal squares snack mix.   ◆

Cookies and Bars

Try our tempting handheld treats.

Nutty Oatmeal-Chocolate Chunk Cookies

Cookies and brownies are quite possibly the perfect sweets. You can hold them in your hand (no plates required), and you can easily package them to send off to a hungry college student or a brave soul serving our country. Whether you like them soft and chewy or prefer them crispier, we've included all your favorites.

Nutty Oatmeal-Chocolate Chunk Cookies

MAKES 6 DOZEN
PREP: 10 MIN., BAKE: 8 MIN. PER BATCH

2½ cups uncooked regular oats
1 cup butter or margarine, softened
1 cup sugar
1 cup firmly packed brown sugar
2 large eggs

1 Tbsp. vanilla extract
2 cups all-purpose flour
1 tsp. baking powder
1 tsp. baking soda
½ tsp. salt
3 (1.55-oz.) milk chocolate
  candy bars, chopped
1½ cups chopped pecans

1. Process oats in a blender or food processor until ground; set aside.
2. Beat 1 cup butter and sugars at medium speed with an electric mixer until fluffy. Add eggs and vanilla, and beat until blended.
3. Combine ground oats, flour, and next 3 ingredients. Add to butter mixture, beating until blended. Stir in chocolate and pecans. Drop dough by tablespoonfuls onto ungreased baking sheets.
4. Bake at 375° for 7 to 8 minutes or until golden brown; remove to wire racks to cool.

Bayou Brownies
MAKES 15 BROWNIES
PREP: 10 MIN., BAKE: 40 MIN.

1 cup chopped pecans
½ cup butter, melted
3 large eggs, divided

1 (18.25-oz.) package yellow
  cake mix
1 (8-oz.) package cream cheese,
  softened
1 (16-oz.) package powdered sugar

1. Combine pecans, butter, 1 egg, and cake mix, stirring until well blended; press in bottom of a lightly greased 13- x 9-inch pan.
2. Combine remaining 2 eggs, cream cheese, and powdered sugar in a large mixing bowl; beat at medium speed with an electric mixer until smooth. Pour cream cheese mixture over cake mix layer.
3. Bake at 325° for 40 minutes or until cheese mixture is set. Let cool completely in pan on a wire rack. Cut into squares.

Gooey Turtle Bars
MAKES 2 DOZEN
PREP: 10 MIN., BAKE: 15 MIN.,
CHILL: 30 MIN.

½ cup butter, melted
1½ cups vanilla wafer crumbs
2 cups (12 oz.) semisweet
  chocolate morsels
1 cup pecan pieces
1 (12-oz.) jar caramel topping

1. Combine butter and wafer crumbs in a 13- x 9-inch pan; press into bottom of pan. Sprinkle with morsels and pecans.
2. Remove lid from caramel topping; microwave at HIGH 1 to 1½ minutes or until hot, stirring after 30 seconds. Drizzle evenly over pecans.
3. Bake at 350° for 12 to 15 minutes or until morsels melt; cool in pan on a wire rack. Cover and chill at least 30 minutes; cut into squares.

Chocolate-Pecan Cookies
MAKES 4½ DOZEN
PREP: 5 MIN., BAKE: 10 MIN.
PER BATCH

1 (18.25-oz.) package
  chocolate or yellow cake mix
½ cup vegetable oil
2 large eggs
1 cup (6 oz.) semisweet
  chocolate morsels
½ cup chopped pecans

1. Beat first 3 ingredients at medium speed with an electric mixer until batter is smooth. Stir in chocolate morsels and pecans. Drop by heaping teaspoonfuls onto ungreased baking sheets.
2. Bake at 350° for 8 to 10 minutes. Remove to wire racks to cool. ▶

Bayou Brownies

PHOTOGRAPHS: RALPH ANDERSON, BETH DREILING, JOHN O'HAGAN / STYLING: LISA POWELL BAILEY, MINDI SHAPIRO LEVINE, ROSE NGUYEN, CARI SOUTH / FOOD STYLING: ANGELA SELLERS

last-minute goodies

Turkey Treats

MAKES 42 TREATS
PREP: 30 MIN.

1 (16-oz.) package cream-filled
    chocolate sandwich cookies
¼ cup red cinnamon candies
1¼ cups malted milk balls
1 (16-oz.) container ready-to-
    spread chocolate frosting
1 (9½-oz.) package candy corn

1. Separate each cookie, leaving cream filling on 1 side; set cookie halves without filling aside.

2. To make turkey body, attach a cinnamon candy (for turkey head) to each malted milk ball (turkey body) with a dab of chocolate frosting. Attach turkey body to cream filling on cookie halves using a dab of chocolate frosting.

3. Spread chocolate frosting on the inside of each remaining plain cookie half. For the turkey tail, arrange candy corn on chocolate-frosting cookies with wide end of candy along outer edge. Attach each turkey tail behind a turkey body using chocolate frosting. Store assembled turkeys in the refrigerator.

Turkey Treats

Peanut Blossom Cookies

MAKES 4 DOZEN
PREP: 10 MIN., BAKE: 10 MIN.
PER BATCH

You'll love these 6-ingredient cookies that are ready in 10 minutes.

1 (14-oz.) can sweetened
    condensed milk
¾ cup creamy peanut
    butter
1 tsp. vanilla extract
2 cups all-purpose baking mix
⅓ cup sugar
1 (9-oz.) package milk
    chocolate kisses

1. Stir together condensed milk, peanut butter, and vanilla, stirring until smooth. Add baking mix, stirring well.

2. Shape dough into 1-inch balls; roll in sugar, and place on ungreased baking sheets. Make an indentation in center of each ball with thumb or spoon handle.

3. Bake at 375° for 8 to 10 minutes or until lightly browned. Remove cookies from oven, and press a chocolate kiss in center of each cookie. Transfer to wire racks to cool completely.

Peanut Blossom Cookies

Raspberry Shortbread

Raspberry Shortbread

MAKES 6 DOZEN
PREP: 15 MIN., BAKE: 20 MIN.
PER BATCH

Rich and buttery, these delectable treats pair perfectly with a cup of hot coffee or tea.

1 cup butter, softened
⅔ cup sugar
2½ cups all-purpose flour
1 (10-oz.) jar seedless raspberry
    jam, divided*
1½ cups powdered sugar
3½ Tbsp. water
½ tsp. almond extract

1. Beat butter and sugar at medium speed with an electric mixer until light and fluffy. Gradually add flour,

Coconut-Macadamia Cookies

make ahead

MAKES 3 DOZEN
PREP: 15 MIN., BAKE: 10 MIN.
PER BATCH

½ cup sugar
½ cup firmly packed light brown
    sugar
½ cup butter or margarine,
    softened
1 large egg
1 tsp. vanilla extract
1¼ cups all-purpose flour
1 cup uncooked quick-
    cooking oats
½ cup sweetened flaked coconut
½ tsp. baking soda
¼ tsp. salt
1 cup coarsely chopped
    macadamia nuts

---

1. Beat first 5 ingredients at medium speed with an electric mixer until fluffy.
2. Combine flour and next 5 ingredients. Add half of flour mixture at a time to sugar mixture, beating at low speed until blended after each addition.
3. Drop dough by heaping teaspoonfuls 2 inches apart onto lightly greased baking sheets.
4. Bake at 350° for 7 to 10 minutes or until edges are golden brown. Cool on baking sheets 1 minute. Remove to wire racks to cool. ▶

beating at low speed until blended. Divide dough into 6 equal portions; roll each portion into a 12- x 1-inch strip. Place strips on lightly greased baking sheets.
2. Make a ½-inch-wide x ¼-inch-deep indentation down center of each strip using the handle of a wooden spoon. Spoon half of raspberry jam evenly into indentations.
3. Bake at 350° for 15 minutes. Remove from oven; spoon remaining jam into indentations. Bake 5 more minutes or until lightly browned.
4. Whisk together powdered sugar, water, and extract; drizzle over warm shortbread. Cut each strip diagonally into 1-inch slices. Cool in pans on wire racks.
*Lemon curd or your favorite flavor of jam may be substituted.

Coconut-Macadamia
Cookies

Pecan-Chocolate Chip Cookies

Ultimate Chocolate Chip Cookies

MAKES ABOUT 5 DOZEN
PREP: 30 MIN., BAKE: 14 MIN.
PER BATCH

make
ahead

¾ cup butter, softened
¾ cup granulated sugar
¾ cup firmly packed dark
  brown sugar
2 large eggs
1½ tsp. vanilla extract

2¼ cups plus 2 Tbsp. all-purpose
  flour
1 tsp. baking soda
¾ tsp. salt
1 (12-oz.) package semisweet
  chocolate morsels

1. Beat butter and sugars at medium speed with an electric mixer until creamy. Add eggs and vanilla, beating until blended.
2. Combine flour, baking soda, and salt in a small bowl; gradually add to butter mixture, beating well. Stir in morsels. Drop by tablespoonfuls onto lightly greased baking sheets.
3. Bake at 350° for 8 to 14 minutes or to desired degree of doneness. Remove to wire racks to cool completely.

Peanut Butter-Chocolate Chip Cookies: Decrease salt to ½ tsp. Add 1 cup creamy peanut butter with butter and sugars. Increase flour to 2½ cups plus 2 Tbsp. Proceed with recipe as directed. (Dough will look a little moist.)

Oatmeal-Raisin-Chocolate Chip Cookies: Reduce flour to 2 cups. Add 1 cup uncooked quick-cooking oats to dry ingredients and 1 cup raisins with chocolate morsels. Proceed with recipe as directed.

Pecan-Chocolate Chip Cookies: Add 1½ cups chopped, toasted pecans with chocolate morsels. Proceed with recipe as directed.

Almond-Toffee-Chocolate Chip Cookies: Reduce chocolate morsels to 1 cup. Add ½ cup slivered toasted almonds and 1 cup almond toffee bits. Proceed with recipe as directed. **Note:** For testing purposes only, we used Hershey's Heath Bits O'Brickle Toffee Bits.

Dark Chocolate Chip Cookies: Substitute 1 (12-oz.) package dark chocolate morsels for semisweet chocolate morsels. Proceed with recipe as directed. **Note:** For testing purposes only, we used Hershey's Special Dark Chips.

Chunky Cherry-Double Chip Cookies: Microwave 1 Tbsp. water and ½ cup dried cherries in a glass bowl at HIGH 30 seconds, stirring once. Let stand 10 minutes. Substitute 1 (12-oz.) package semisweet chocolate chunks for morsels. Add 1 cup white chocolate morsels, ⅓ cup slivered toasted almonds, and cherries with chocolate chunks. Proceed with recipe as directed.

Coconut-Macadamia Chunk Cookies: Substitute 1 (12-oz.) package semisweet chocolate chunks for morsels. Add 1 cup white chocolate morsels, ½ cup sweetened flaked coconut, and ½ cup macadamia nuts with chocolate chunks. Proceed with recipe as directed.

Double Chocolate Brownies

MAKES 32 BROWNIES
PREP: 15 MIN., BAKE: 40 MIN.

make ahead

2 (1-oz.) squares unsweetened chocolate
2 (1-oz.) squares semisweet chocolate
1 cup butter, softened
2 cups sugar
4 large eggs
1 cup all-purpose flour
½ tsp. salt
1 tsp. vanilla extract
¾ cup toasted chopped pecans
¾ cup semisweet chocolate morsels

1. Microwave chocolate squares in a small microwave-safe bowl at MEDIUM (50% power) for 30-second intervals until melted (about 1½ minutes total time). Stir chocolate until smooth.

2. Beat butter and sugar at medium speed with an electric mixer until light and fluffy. Add eggs, 1 at a time, beating just until blended after each addition. Add melted chocolate, beating just until blended.

3. Add flour and salt, beating at low speed just until blended. Stir in vanilla, ½ cup pecans, and ½ cup chocolate morsels. Spread batter into a greased and floured 13- x 9-inch baking pan. Sprinkle with remaining ¼ cup pecans and ¼ cup chocolate morsels.

4. Bake at 350° for 40 minutes or until set. Cool completely on a wire rack.

Double Chocolate Brownies With Caramel Frosting: Prepare Double Chocolate Brownies as directed. Melt ¾ cup butter in a large saucepan over low heat. Stir in 2 cups sugar, ½ cup buttermilk, 12 large marshmallows, 1 Tbsp. light corn syrup, and ½ tsp. baking soda. Cook over medium heat, stirring occasionally, 20 to 25 minutes or until a candy thermometer registers 234° (soft-ball stage). Remove from heat, and pour mixture immediately into a large mixing bowl. Beat mixture with an electric mixer at high speed 5 minutes or until mixture thickens and begins to lose its gloss. Spread frosting evenly over brownies. ◆

8 min.   *10 min.*   *12 min.*   *14 min.*

Bake Ultimate Chocolate Chip Cookies 8 minutes for soft and chewy or up to 14 minutes for crispy cookies.

recipe index

Invent Your Own Casserole

This mix-and-match chart takes the guesswork out of creating your own casseroles. You know which foods and flavor combinations your family prefers, so put that knowledge to good use. Simply stir the ingredients together, and bake.

Choose one Sauce Maker.

Choose one Meat or Poultry.

Choose one Vegetable.

Choose one Pasta or Rice.

Choose one or two Toppings.

Invent Your Own Casserole

MAKES 6 SERVINGS
PREP: 15 MIN.; BAKE: 1 HR., 20 MIN.

1 (8-oz.) carton sour cream
1 cup milk
1 cup low-sodium chicken, beef, or
   vegetable broth
1 tsp. salt
1 tsp. pepper

1. Combine 1 cup sour cream, 1 cup milk, 1 cup broth, 1 tsp. salt, 1 tsp. pepper, and desired Sauce Maker (omit sour cream and milk when using tomatoes). Stir in 1 Meat/Poultry, 1 Pasta/Rice, 1 Vegetable, and, if desired, Extras.
2. Spoon casserole mixture into a lightly greased 13- x 9-inch baking dish, and sprinkle with your choice of Toppings.
3. Bake, covered, at 350° for 1 hour and 10 minutes; uncover and bake 10 additional minutes.
Chicken Casserole: Cream of chicken soup, chicken, rice, broccoli, Parmesan cheese, and breadcrumbs.
Ham Casserole: Cream of celery soup, ham, wide egg noodles, Italian green beans, garlic, and 2 portions Swiss cheese.
Turkey Casserole: Italian-style diced tomatoes, turkey, medium pasta shells, spinach, onion, garlic, mozzarella cheese, and breadcrumbs.
Vegetarian Casserole: Italian-style diced tomatoes, rice, yellow squash, olives, 4 portions celery, 4 portions bell pepper, garlic, Parmesan cheese, and breadcrumbs. ◆

Choose 1 Sauce Maker:

1 (10¾-oz.) can cream of
   mushroom soup
1 (10¾-oz.) can cream of
   celery soup
1 (10¾-oz.) can cream of
   chicken soup
2 (14½-oz.) cans Italian-style
   diced tomatoes, undrained

Choose 1 Pasta/Rice:

2 cups uncooked elbow macaroni
1 cup uncooked long-grain rice
4 cups uncooked wide egg
   noodles
3 cups uncooked medium shells
3 cups torn flour or corn tortillas

Choose 1 or more Extras (optional):

1 (15-oz.) can white beans, rinsed
   and drained
1 (7.3-oz.) jar sliced mushrooms,
   drained
1 (3-oz.) can sliced ripe olives
½ cup chopped roasted red
   bell peppers
¼ cup chopped bell pepper
¼ cup chopped onion
¼ cup chopped celery
2 garlic cloves, minced
1 (4.5-oz.) can chopped
   green chiles
1 (1¼-oz.) envelope taco
   seasoning mix

Choose 1 Meat/Poultry:

2 cups chopped cooked chicken
2 cups chopped cooked ham
2 cups chopped cooked turkey
2 cups shredded barbecued pork
   or chicken
1 lb. ground beef, browned and
   drained

Choose 1 Vegetable:

1 (10-oz.) package frozen chopped
   spinach, thawed
1 (10-oz.) package frozen cut
   broccoli
1 (10-oz.) package frozen Italian
   green beans
1 (10-oz.) package frozen English
   peas
1 (16-oz.) package frozen sliced
   yellow squash
1 (10-oz.) package frozen whole
   kernel corn
1 (10-oz.) package frozen mixed
   vegetables

Choose 1 or 2 Toppings:

½ cup (2 oz.) shredded
   mozzarella cheese
½ cup (2 oz.) shredded Swiss
   cheese
½ cup grated Parmesan cheese
½ cup (2 oz.) shredded Mexican
   cheese blend
½ cup fine, dry breadcrumbs

PHOTOGRAPH: RALPH ANDERSON / STYLING: JESSICA KRONBERG / FOOD STYLING: ANGELA SELLERS